THE HIDDEN POWER OF
BLEND MODES
IN ADOBE® PHOTOSHOP®

SCOTT VALENTINE

Adobe

THE HIDDEN POWER OF BLEND MODES IN ADOBE® PHOTOSHOP®
Scott Valentine

Adobe Press books are published by:

PEACHPIT
1249 Eighth Street
Berkeley, CA 94710
510/524-2178
800/283-9444

Peachpit is a division of Pearson Education.
For the latest on Adobe Press books, go to www.adobepress.com.
To report errors, please send a note to errata@peachpit.com.

Adobe Press Editor: Victor Gavenda
Project Editor: Nancy Peterson
Editor: Bob Lindstrom
Technical Editor: Rocky Berlier
Production Coordinator: Becky Winter
Copy Editor: Darren Meiss
Compositor: Danielle Foster
Indexer: Jack Lewis
Cover design and photo collage: Mimi Heft
Interior design: Mimi Heft

ISBN 13: 978-0-321-82376-2
ISBN 10:   0-321-82376-1

9 8 7 6 5 4 3 2 1

Printed and bound in the United States of America

For my wife, Carla, and our own little blend, Austin.

TABLE OF CONTENTS

Foreword x

PART I   BLEND MODE BASICS   1

CHAPTER 1
INTRODUCTION   3

How Blend Modes Work 5
Conventions Used in the Book 8
What You Need to Know 8
Using a Digital Tablet 9
Getting More from Blend Modes 10
Thanks 11

CHAPTER 2
GENERAL TECHNIQUES   13

Blending In 14
The Basics 14
Combining Blends 16
Painting 19
Blending Layers 22
Layer Styles 24

Apply Image and Calculations 25
Smart Objects. 26
Building Reference Images 27

PART II CREATIVE TECHNIQUES   33

CHAPTER 3
PHOTOGRAPHY   35

Matt Kloskowski: The Four Blend Modes You
  Need the Most 37
Remove Color Cast 38
Bright Eyes. 39
Dodge and Burn 40
Mark Heaps: Luminosity to the Rescue 43
Edge Contrast 45
Gray Day Recovery. 46
Remove Vignetting 49
Chris Tarantino: Calculations 51
Vignettes. 55
Zone Control with Gradients 56
High Pass Sharpening 1 58
High Pass Sharpening 2 59
Katrin Eismann: Smart Filters and Blend Modes 60
Saturation and Luminosity Curves 63

CHAPTER 4
PHOTOGRAPHIC MANIPULATION & COMPOSITING 65

Julieanne Kost: Textures and Color 67
Portrait Tone and Contrast 69
Sepia/Color Toning 70
Hand Tinting 71
Sketched Lines 1 73
Sketched Lines 2 75
RC Concepcion: Divide for Textures 76
Soft Glow 1. 79
Trapping "Blend If" Transparency. 80
Adjustment Layer Noise 81
Graphic Illustration 83
Soft Glow 2 85
Pixelated Edges 87
Carrie Beene: Custom Lens Flare & Glow. 89
Hard Mix Contrast 90
Hard Mix Noise. 91
Hard Mix Noise Variations 93
Gentle Rain 1 95
Gentle Rain 2 97
Calvin Hollywood: Freaky Amazing Details 99

CHAPTER 5
DESIGN, PAINTING, & ILLUSTRATION 101

Kat Gilbert: 3D & Fine Art 103

Custom Brushes 1 106

John Shannon: Illustrating with Color 109

3D: Depth Maps 113

Funky Difference Gradients 115

Chris Georgenes: Illustrated Textures 117

Glowing Lines and Dust 120

Jim Tierney: Random Differences 122

Classic Illustration Shading 125

Steve Caplin: Illustrated Gloss 127

Patterns: Checkerboard 128

Patterns: Retro Lines 129

Crosshatch Textures 130

Patterns: More Squares 131

Patrick LaMontagne: Dodge and Burn for Grown-ups 133

PART III   BLEND MODES IN DEPTH   135

CHAPTER 6
DECODING BLEND MODES   137
Understanding the Listings. 138
Reference Images 139

CHAPTER 7
LIST OF BLEND MODES   145
Normal 146
Dissolve 147
Darken 148
Multiply 150
Color Burn 151
Linear Burn 152
Darker Color 153
Lighten 155
Screen 156
Color Dodge. 157
Linear Dodge (Add) 158
Lighter Color 159
Overlay. 160
Soft Light 161
Hard Light 162
Vivid Light 163
Linear Light 164
Pin Light. 165
Hard Mix 166
Difference. 167
Exclusion 168
Subtract. 169
Divide 170
Hue 172
Saturation. 173
Color 174
Luminosity. 175
Other Blend Modes. 176

PART IV APPENDICES   181

APPENDIX A
COLOR MODES AND BIT DEPTH   183

APPENDIX B
BLEND MODES REFERENCE TABLE   187

APPENDIX C
ONLINE RESOURCES   193

APPENDIX D
BLEND MODE TOOLS MATRIX   197

INDEX   200

FOREWORD

To paraphrase Einstein, "Science without art is lame; art without science is blind." At its best, Photoshop blends math, art—and heart.

You'll find all three in Scott Valentine, and in his merry band of contributors to this book.

To write poetry, you'd best understand grammar. Featuring well over 500 menu commands and dozens of tools, Photoshop can appear overwhelming, but like any language, it can be broken down into a series of parts. Understand how those parts relate, and you can do nearly anything.

In the language of Photoshop, blending modes are like adverbs: They govern how something is done, often making a night-and-day difference.

With their often inscrutable names (what the heck is "Linear Dodge (Add)," complete with parenthesis?), blending modes can draw blank stares from even seasoned Photoshop vets. These mathematical formulae, however, are vital to producing things as "simple" as the common drop shadow effect. So, how does one efficiently grok enough theory (but not too much), while keeping the focus on real-world results?

That's where Scott comes in. Much to the envy of us arts-and-letters-only types, Scott combines a technical mind (he's trained as a physicist) with the down-to-earth generosity of a great teacher. These qualities have won him the support of more than a dozen industry luminaries (Julieanne Kost, Eismann, RC Concepcion, Matt Kloskowski, and Calvin Hollywood, to name a few) who have contributed tips and recipes to this book.

Aimed at intermediate users—but with enough info to get beginners up to speed plus a few advanced tricks for the pros—*The Hidden Power of Blend Modes* will have you saying "Wow, I didn't know Photoshop could do that (or, at least, could do it that quickly)."

Happy blending,

John Nack

PART I
BLEND MODE BASICS

Get up to speed with the fundamentals of how Adobe Photoshop blend modes work and the best ways to use them effectively.

CHAPTER 1
INTRODUCTION

This chapter explains some general concepts that you'll need to understand as you get started with blend modes in Photoshop CS6.

Normal
Dissolve
Darken
Multiply
Color Burn
Linear Burn
Darker Color
Lighten
Screen
Color Dodge
Linear Dodge (Add)
Lighter Color
Overlay
Soft Light
Hard Light
Vivid Light
Linear Light
Pin Light
Hard Mix
Difference
Exclusion
Subtract
Divide
Hue
Saturation
Color
Luminosity

Why write a book about blend modes? Doesn't the Photoshop® world, by and large, know what they do? As it turns out, no. Most users, even those proficient in digital editing and artwork, have a few favorite modes they rely on. But when they venture outside of those three or four favorites, they are usually just flipping switches to see what they like. (I do this a lot myself, especially when I don't really know what I want.)

Also, blend modes are pervasive. Photography, special effects, graphic design, and even painting—they all have blending modes lurking around somewhere. Chances are you already use them frequently, but may not give them much thought. It's time to change that.

As you'll see in the guest entries in this book, top Photoshop experts have their own secret sauces and reasons for using blend modes. Some uses may seem simple, but that simplicity is the result of significant exploration. Other uses are fairly complicated, stacking layer after layer of detailed operations. Most methods, however, are somewhere in between—utilizing lots of power and flexibility but in only a few steps that are not always obvious.

Personally, I find myself turning to blend modes to meet a variety of imaging challenges. Whether blending, correcting, or tweaking, I nearly always throw some blend mode power into the mix.

This book is intended to make blend modes comfortable and frequently used, the way *you* would use them. I've organized the techniques into three major sections to accommodate all kinds of digital artists from photographers to illustrators, from painters to designers. And if you're a member of the ever-expanding group of artists who cross these boundaries, you should feel right at home.

Most of the techniques are not just combinations of blend modes, but combine multiple resources while featuring blend modes as a core component. You will be mixing and matching many tools and approaches, such as adjustment layers and filters, brush tools, and even channels. Every technique is aimed at flexibility and meeting real-world challenges.

That is not to imply that this book represents an exhaustive study of all possible blend mode techniques. Due to space and time considerations, I had to choose which methods to show, and which to save for another time.

Some popular and well-known techniques have been omitted from this text. Specifically, noise reduction techniques are omitted here. Newer cameras and third-party software, as well as Photoshop's native tools and those in Camera Raw, do a much better job in this arena than all the blending techniques I've seen (with the possible exception of hand-painting).

HOW BLEND MODES WORK

When you get right down to it, blend modes are equations. They take input values, do something to them, and give you an output. In the simplest case of a Photoshop image with two layers, each layer is input, the top layer's blend mode is the equation (or function), and you see the output on your display.

For blend modes to work, we need at least two layers in Photoshop. The techniques in this book refer to the bottom layer as the "base," and the top layer as the "blend." The blend layer is the one whose blend mode controls the output.

It's worth noting that the blending process does not change the actual inputs. The blend mode affects only the image rendered to the screen. In this sense, the output is *virtual*: it's not actually written to the file when you save your document. Here's an example to illustrate this:

When you peer through a piece of stained glass, the image you perceive looks different (**1.1**). Looking through a chunk of green glass, for example, a plain white wall will appear green, even though the wall color hasn't actually changed. What's different when using this *colored filter* is the light passing through the tinted glass.

NOTE The idea of the output being virtual is subtle, but important. When you stack multiple blend modes and adjustment layers, the order in which the effects are applied starts from the bottom of the layers stack and goes up. Any changes you make to the lower stacks get propagated up through the stack, changing the inputs all the way.

1.1 A color filter blocks some colors without changing the source colors.

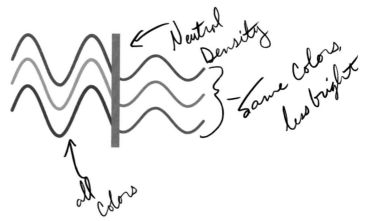

1.2 A neutral filter changes the perceived balance of the source colors.

NOTE In Photoshop, a filter changes the actual pixels on a layer, typically by moving them around and possibly changing colors. Because this works unlike the optical filter in our "green glass" analogy, I will use the phrase '"Photoshop filters" to distinguish them from standard more general "filters."

Has the light itself changed? Not in the physical world, as it turns out. The green glass simply blocks everything that isn't green and lets only the green light pass. While this is a very simplified description, it describes basically how a *filter* works: It allows some elements to pass through while blocking others.

Filters come in many types. When you're looking through the gray lenses of sunglasses (**1.2**)—or a neutral density filter, if you're a photographer—you're using a *neutral filter*. That type of filter reduces the intensity of light in general, but all colors remain visible.

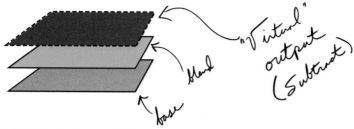

1.3 Blend modes also act to block or pass certain colors.

1.4 Some blend modes achieve results by comparing pixels.

Blend modes appear to behave in a similar way when they act to block or pass certain colors. The Color blend mode, for example, does behave this way, and seems to block everything but the top layer's color (**1.3**). But blend modes can, of course, be much more complex. For example, some compare two pixels on adjacent layers and change their behavior based on the color or brightness of each (**1.4**).

Blend modes have two interesting features that should encourage you to experiment.

First, they do not change the file size of your document by themselves. Adding layers does increase file size, but changing the blend modes of existing layers does not. The sneaky addition to that is adjustment layers. They add very little to file size, and they can have blend modes applied to them. You'll find more detail on adjustment layers in Chapter 2, "General Techniques."

Second, blend modes are nondestructive. Because they are just instructions that alter your display output, you can change them whenever you like. They won't change the data on your layer, and you don't have to worry about losing your work.

NOTE Remember that blend modes take their inputs from values at specific pixel locations. If you consider that each layer in a Photoshop file is really a grid of pixels, and the contents of that layer can be moved around, it's easy to understand that each location can have unique information in it. As a result, a blend mode's output may look different as you move layer contents around and change the pixel-specific inputs of each layer.

1.5 A glance at the interface shows the basic structure of a blend mode technique.

CONVENTIONS USED IN THE BOOK

As you read this book, you'll find that many of the explanations repeat information. Experienced users may be able to simply glance at the layer stack screen shot (**1.5**) and get what they need. Readers who are less familiar with Photoshop may want to read the entire description and indulge in a little "try it and see." I've also included summary steps when I think they're useful to performing the technique.

In general, I've avoided providing specifics because every image will be different. Some techniques include a brief discussion on selecting good candidate images for a particular look, while others describe variations you can try depending on the image and your desired outcome.

In *all* cases, however, you should see each entry as a starting point. With an infinite number of possible images and an infinite set of possible outcomes, there is no way that one book (or even a library of books) could cover every variation.

All the screen shots were taken in Photoshop CS6 on a Mac, so a Windows-based interface will look a little different. Whenever possible, I noted any tools or techniques that are specific to one version of Adobe Photoshop. Similarly, when keyboard shortcuts vary between Mac OS and Windows, I've noted the difference.

WHAT YOU NEED TO KNOW

To keep this book concise and broadly useful, I made some assumptions about what users should know before exploring these techniques. Beginners can certainly make use of this book, and I hope this introduction serves as a solid foundation for beginning and intermediate users.

So what should you know to get the most of out this book? You should be familiar with (not an expert on) the following:

- General layers operations, including creating and renaming layers, applying layer styles, and using masks

- How to make selections, and how to save those selections to a new layer or alpha channel

- Brushes, selection tools, and the options bar for later versions of Photoshop
- How to apply a filter from the menu and adjust its parameters
- Creating and editing gradients
- Using keyboard shortcuts

To take advantage of the more advanced techniques, you'll additionally need to know:

- How to use channels and what they represent
- Clipping layers
- How to create and edit Smart Objects and Smart Filters

After all of this, there is one absolute requirement you must have to get anything useful out of this book: curiosity. Everything presented here is a tiny slice of what *could be*. It's up to you to experiment and push beyond these examples and techniques. Consider each a starting point, and maybe just a piece of a much larger effort. Own what you do with this information, and enhance these techniques with your own creative spark.

USING A DIGITAL TABLET

Many of the techniques in this book rely on fine adjustments, and some make use of painting tools. To get precision and to save some strain on your wrists, I highly recommend getting a digital tablet (**1.6**).

1.6 A digital tablet permits additional accuracy and prevents wrist strain.

Aside from a computer and Adobe Photoshop, if I didn't have a digital tablet, I really couldn't get my work done. Wacom's (wacom.com) Intuos line is my favorite of the tablet options available.

I started this book with my trusty Intuos4, but switched to Intuos5 for the last month or so of writing. It's like my computer's trackpad grew up and added a pen. Digital tablets are meant to give you a more natural input method by using a pen, and with the Intuos5, your fingers. This creates a very comfortable experience, and also increases your ability to make detailed edits with amazing precision.

If you spend much time editing digital images, you should seriously consider a tablet. Ergonomically, they allow a more comfortable hand position, and get your entire arm involved, which is a key factor in avoiding the repetitive stress of using trackballs and mice (which I also use for standard office-type work).

GETTING MORE FROM BLEND MODES

The single biggest thing you can do to further your knowledge of blend modes is to use them. Experiment, tinker, and fiddle with the knobs. As you build your Photoshop experience, you should approach most challenges by first defining them because defining a problem often defines much of the solution.

A great exercise is to pick one blend mode and take it out for a spin. See what it can do. Look for overall effects as well as details. Once you pick up on something, spend a little time digging in. Make notes, and try the same trick or steps on different images. Ask yourself what works, what you like, and what you don't like.

For additional help, look to online forums. You'll find many community-driven discussion boards, some sponsored by professional organizations and training companies. Adobe has its own community at forums.adobe.com. And don't forget about sites that have focused themes, such as photography and illustration.

In addition to the techniques on using blend modes that you'll learn in Section II of this book, you can find additional techniques on my site, lightningsymphony.com/hpobm.

THANKS

Even though I wrote this book, I could not have done it without the help of some amazing people. At the top of my list to thank are my wife, Carla, and son, Austin, whose patience seems to know no bounds. I love you!

Next, the editing and and design crew at Peachpit who made this an enjoyable experience. Victor, Nancy, Bob, and Darren all conspired to turn out a top-notch work. Mimi, Becky, and Danielle were responsible for the look and layout, which I think is just amazing and beautiful. And I want to set aside a special mention for Rocky who did the technical editing, without whose amazing insight and encouragement during planning I might have given up.

From Adobe, senior Computer Scientist and Photoshop engineer (since 1996!) Chris Cox and Product Manager Zorana Gee were great on technical questions and helped me understand things well enough to explain them here.

To those who contributed their time and expertise in providing the guest entries, I am honored and humbled to have you as a part of this work. You are my heroes.

A big thank-you goes out to the Photoshop community at large, but especially to the Photoshop and Lightroom group on Facebook (pshopandlightroom). Many of these folks were lab rats for some of my crazier ideas. They're always willing to help out.

A large part of why I love Adobe Photoshop so much is the people it brings together. Users, developers, artists, photographers, trainers—people who are passionate about this fantastic tool give rise to creative voices around the globe. That includes people like you.

CHAPTER 2
GENERAL
TECHNIQUES

To make full use of blend modes, you should have a handful of methods ready in your toolbox. Combine them, remix them, build on them, and make something beautiful.

2.1 Changing the opacity on a Linear Light layer changes the High Pass filter's effect.

BLENDING IN

A main goal of this book is to become so familiar with blend modes that you no longer need to "try it and see," even though that is a valid approach, especially when you are not sure exactly which look or effect you want. To get started, however, you need to know some general methods for working with blend modes, along with some basic facts.

First, recognize that these layer-based tools are largely nondestructive. You can use any or all of them with impunity—you are not changing any aspect of your image that you cannot change back.

There are exceptions. Painting tools can have a blend mode applied as pixels are laid down or modified. The Dodge, Burn, and Sponge tools blend destructively on the target pixels (although there are ways around this).

Second, some blend modes are sensitive to opacity. As you lower opacity or apply masks, you may see subtle, sometimes unexpected changes. A startling example of this occurs when using Linear Light on an inverted High Pass layer. With larger values of the High Pass slider, the effect ranges from a soft blur at lower opacity to an outline at higher opacity (**2.1**).

Third, blend modes are scattered throughout Photoshop. You can find them on layers; in tools such as Fill, Stroke, Calculations, and Apply; and in layer styles. In fact, most layer styles are based on, or make heavy use of blend modes.

THE BASICS

The following general techniques offer so many possibilities that I recommend you take notes as you explore them. Oftentimes, the same general steps can produce dramatically different outcomes simply by changing some of the image elements or swapping the order of operations.

Some general techniques are used repeatedly throughout this book. These techniques are important to develop independent of the recipes you will find later. Some of my favorites are:

- Basic self blend (**2.2**)

  Duplicate the base layer and change the blend mode of the duplicate.

- Inverted self blend

  As the name implies, the base is duplicated and the duplicate is inverted by pressing Ctrl+I (Windows) or Command+I (Mac).

- Filtered self blend

  Similar to a basic self blend, but the duplicated layer is manipulated with a filter, such as a blur.

- Fill blend

  A blank layer is added above the blend layer and completely filled with a solid color or gradient.

- Selection blend

  A selection is made from the base layer and then duplicated or filled on a new layer. The selection can be as simple as a marquee selection, or can be the result of complex processes that were stored as an alpha channel.

- Painting blend

  Similar to a fill blend, but the pixels are painted directly onto a layer.

- Adjustment blend (**2.3**)

  Adjustment layers can take blend modes, too. Many such layers behave as if you performed a self blend, but allow you to change the adjustment values. When used properly, this is a great way to save some file space and keep things a bit more organized.

2.2 The Background layer is duplicated for a self blend.

2.3 Applying a Luminosity blend to an unchanged Curves adjustment is the same as applying the blend mode to a duplicate of the Background layer.

TIP As you record your journeys, note how the same technique may require changes or create a new effect depending on the input image.

TIP Layers can be clipped to other layers by holding down the Alt (Windows) or Option (Mac) key and clicking between two layers; by pressing Alt+Ctrl+G or Option+Command+G; or by choosing Layer > Create Clipping Mask. The clipped (top) layer then affects only the layer immediately beneath it. Adjustment layers can be assigned to individual layers in this manner.

To make the most of these basic techniques, here are some tips to give you additional control and finesse over blend modes:

- Use the Blend If sliders to selectively adjust transparency between layers.

- Examine your channels to see if any interesting selections can be made, and determine how much each color contributes to your overall image.

- Use the Opacity slider to reduce the intensity of a blending layer.

- Take advantage of the Fade Filter option, outlined in the Blending Effects section of this chapter.

- Blending layers can be stacked, combined, masked, and adjusted to create more intricate effects.

- Paint strokes placed on a layer by themselves can be blurred and filtered, take layer effects, and so on.

2.4 The Orton effect (described later in the book) uses several duplicated and blurred layers with different blend modes.

COMBINING BLENDS

Many blend modes can be used by themselves as simple effects or tools, but they can also be combined in several ways, or used temporarily as a foundation for another effect.

A common approach is to stack layers with different blend modes. An example of this is the Orton, or soft-glow effect.

This effect uses three layers (bottom to top): Normal, Screen, and Lighten or Overlay (**2.4**). The two blended layers are given a special treatment in addition to the mode change. The first layer is duplicated then blurred to the point where almost all detail is lost, and only major areas of color remain. This layer is duplicated, and desaturated for the top layer. Because the first layer retains color, the Screen blend gives some overlapping color and softness. The Overlay layer acts as a Dodge and Burn layer, selectively brightening or darkening the same color areas. Opacity is lowered to give more control over the effect (**2.5**).

2.5 Lower the opacity value to have more control over the effect.

2.6 The edges that result from this blend can be committed by merging the layers, or preferably, by using the Claw key combination to copy the visible layers to a new layer.

TIP To keep a snapshot of the currently visible layers, use one of my favorite shortcuts, the "Claw." Press Ctrl+Alt+Shift+E (Windows) or Command+Option+Shift+E (Mac) to copy a merged version of whatever is visible to the new layer.

The result is a glowing, soft-edged look—but not all images will behave the same way. The image content determines whether this effect is useful or not. Good image candidates for this look will include large areas of light, or a strong directional source that complements a glowing surface. Details are important so that this look doesn't simply wash out. By adding a noise layer or other textures, you can tease even more looks out of this combination.

Individually blending these modes allows you to control saturation, dodge/burn looks, add further effects, and much more. Your image is still nondestructively edited because you filtered duplicates; so you can wipe out your changes and start over, or save one version in a grouped folder to later compare it with other looks you apply to the image. You can also simply change the blend mode on each layer.

Now, there are other ways to get a similar look, but most take much more time and involve painting or delicate masking. Those approaches have their merits so do not exclude them! But what we have done here is let the image itself do the hard work—instead of painting a complex mask for highlights and shadows, we have extracted the information we need and told it how to behave.

Another way to combine blend modes is to *commit* them, or make them permanent. Sometimes it is difficult to use the output of a blend mode because that output is dynamic. For example, suppose you wanted to capture the difference between a layer and its slightly blurred copy to generate an edge mask. You would start by duplicating the layer, adding a tiny blur, and then setting the blurred layer to Difference mode. Depending on the amount of blur, you could get some nice edges in color where there are differences, and black everywhere else (**2.6**). See "Saving Blend Mode Outputs" for details.

Layer groups have a special way of combining blend modes using Pass Through, which appears in the drop-down menu only when a group is selected in the Layers panel. Pass Through treats the group as if it were part of the normal layer stack, allowing adjustments and blend modes that are applied to individual layers to affect everything beneath them. However, setting a group's blend mode to anything other than Pass Through causes the group to behave like a single, merged image.

In other words, if a layer group includes two layers, with the top layer set to Divide, Pass Through would allow the Divide layer to affect all layers below it in the stack, including the layer immediately beneath it within the group. But if the group blend mode were changed to Normal, the Divide layer would affect *only* the layer beneath it in the group and nothing else.

PAINTING

The Brush tool and its variants can also be used with blend modes. When you create a blank layer set to Normal blending and choose the Brush tool, you have the option to change the tool's blend mode and opacity independently of the layer.

Not all of the Brush tools use the same set of modes, and not all are applied in the same way. Many of the tools, such as the Clone Stamp, have some blending options, but they are of limited utility and generally apply the same way that painting behaves by acting only on those pixels on the currently active layer.

Let's start with the Brush tool itself, which is typically used for painting or drawing. Regardless of the tool's blend mode, only the Opacity setting will interact with layers beneath the currently active layer. For example, consider a document with a photograph in the background and one blank layer set to Normal

2.7 The Brush tool's blend mode can be changed independently of the layer's blend mode.

2.8 Strokes with different blend modes that overlap on the same layer behave as if they were made on different layers with blend modes then merged.

NOTE Mixer brushes do not use blend modes, but that doesn't stop you from using multiple layers with different modes.

above it in the layer stack. If you select the Brush tool (B) and set the tool blend mode to Difference with 100% Opacity, painting on the blank layer looks as if you painted in Normal mode. In fact, if you make a continuous stroke that overlaps itself, the paint still behaves as if it is set to Normal mode.

When you stop the stroke (such as when picking up a stylus or releasing the mouse button), a new stroke can be created. The new stroke will interact with the previous one based on the tool's blend mode. However, the new pixels still do not interact with the photographic layer beneath.

Lowering the opacity of the brush certainly does allow some of the photo to show through. This also holds true for the Dissolve blend mode when the Brush tool's marker (the shape of the brush) has soft, transparent elements. The transparent areas of the brush will show the Dissolve blend mode effect.

The main point is that you can use all the available blend modes for the Brush tool at any given moment, so long as you are not currently in the middle of a stroke. Put another way, you can paint a yellow line with Overlay, choose red and change the blend mode to Hard Light for the next stroke, and change yet again for the next, all on the same layer. These strokes will interact with each other.

By painting with modes applied to the Brush tool, you can easily get some beautifully organic and graphic looks. Furthermore, you can combine the output of Brush tool blending with layer blending (**2.7**).

After you've painted some pixels on the blank layer, they are committed in that they do not preserve the memory of the blend mode they were painted with. Only the *result* of the blending contributes to the image (**2.8**).

In other words, when you overlap two strokes, the overlapping areas show the result of the blending modes. But the result is *rendered*, or made permanent. You cannot go back and change the blend mode of a stroke that has already been laid down. The results of the overlap are now permanent. However, at any point you can change the layer's blend mode.

Normal

Multiply

Hard Mix

Exclusion

2.9 A simple test can demonstrate the behavior of overlapping strokes.

To see how this works, try the following steps:

1. Fill a layer with a gradient, and then create a new blank layer on top of the solid one.

2. Using the brush, choose a round brush tip with a soft edge. Create a vertical stroke at 100% opacity starting with Normal blend mode, and then paint another stroke next to the first, changing to Multiply, Linear Light, and so on (**2.9**). Choose any four or five you like and make several lines. If you do not overlap any of the pixels, even the soft edges, you will not see any difference between strokes. The exception is Dissolve mode as noted earlier.

3. Change the layer's blend mode to Hard Light, for example. Lower the opacity of the layer. All the strokes behave the same way regardless of the tool's blend mode when they were painted.

4. Return to Normal mode for both the Brush tool and the layer, and bring opacity of both to 100%. Make one stroke across the top that crosses the original lines. Not surprisingly, you get a straight line that doesn't appear to interact with the others.

5. Do the same thing a little lower with the mode set to something different. Choose Hard Mix and see what you get. Where the strokes overlap, the mode controls the interaction, but between overlapping areas, the stroke ignores the layer beneath. Now change the layer blend mode to Multiply.

When working with tool and layer blends, the paint strokes interact with each other, but the overall layer blending is independent. It makes for some non-intuitive methods, but once you get the hang of it, you can pull off some incredible techniques.

Some tools have the option to include all visible layers or only the underlying layers. While these tools, such as the Clone Stamp, also allow you to change the blend modes, they again only have an effect on pixels that are actually on the layer.

Also note that these same characteristics apply to gradients, an effect we'll use in a few recipes.

BLENDING LAYERS

Sometimes you will want to combine several effects or looks. Getting multiple elements to interact or blend together can be tricky, but a couple of available tools help with this.

OPACITY VS. FILL

2.10 Lowering the Fill value preserves the layer style, a drop shadow, in this case. Note that the *paint* pixels are now transparent.

At first glance, Opacity and Fill seem to do the same thing, but there is one important distinction. Opacity changes the entire layer, so all pixels are equally adjusted as you move the slider. Fill, on the other hand, does not affect layer styles. For example, when you create text on a layer and then add a drop shadow, you can lower the Fill option so that only the drop shadow shows (**2.10**).

You can then refine the look by lowering the overall opacity. This is a great technique for adding watermarks and controlling subtle special effects.

Some blend modes also react differently to Fill vs. Opacity due to the way the blend modes use alpha, or transparency, information. One example of this is Hard Mix, which is used in a few recipes.

2.11 The Fade dialog box showing a drop-down menu in which you can select the blend mode and adjust opacity with the slider.

TIP You can choose Edit > Fade, or press Ctrl+Shift+F or Command+Shift+F.

FADE

You can apply a blend mode immediately after some operations using the Fade command, which gives you a slight workaround to the restriction of using only one blend mode on a layer (**2.11**).

Using Fade, you can apply a filter to a layer, and then mitigate or alter that effect by using a blend mode and opacity. With this operation, you are combining the steps of duplicating the layer, applying a filter, changing that duplicate's blend mode and opacity, blending it with itself, and then merging everything. You're basically creating a merged self blend in a single dialog box.

This technique produces some interesting looks, but in the end, is nothing significantly different than what you'd get by following the manual steps. Still, it's a great way to apply committed blends with filters while saving a little time and space.

So why is this interesting? Because you can now change the blend mode of the result! You didn't have to make another duplicate and use the "Claw" to get another blending layer copy. While this varies from the prior claim of being non-destructive, it is certainly useful and can reduce file size.

BLEND IF

The tool I use almost as frequently as layers themselves is Blend If. It is essentially a parametric luminosity blend with sliders to let you selectively adjust opacity based on input from either the current layer or the one beneath it.

When you open up the Layer Style dialog box by double-clicking a layer thumbnail, the first panel you get is Blending Options (**2.12**). At the bottom of this view is the Blend If section, which consists of two rows of sliders with split triangles.

Once you start playing with these sliders, they're pretty easy to figure out visually. Behind the scenes, pixels are turned off based on their absolute values as determined by the slider. The input value can come from the current layer, or from the visible elements beneath it. Put another way, a given set of pixels can be turned off based on their own color as determined by the slider, or the pixels above that color in the bottom layer. Choosing "This Layer" makes the decision using colors in the current layer, but choosing "Underlying Layer" turns off pixels in the current layer that are directly above the selected color or range from the underlying layer.

NOTE The thin line in the slider handles indicates that you can split them by holding down Alt/Option and grabbing one half of the slider. So, instead of having a hard threshold, you can now have a soft transition between blended and unblended values.

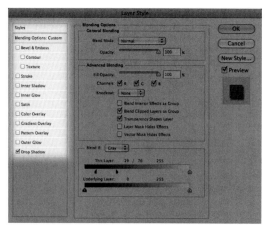

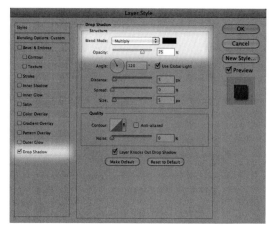

2.12 **2.13**

The values are RGB or Gray depending on which you choose from the drop-down menu. You can combine these in any way you like, so you are not limited, for example, to adjusting the Red values.

You can use Blend If to stack layer blends that may not otherwise get you the precise look you want. For example, you may find a recipe that gives you the perfect tone in the mids and bright areas, but darkens your shadows far too much. Using Blend If, you can reveal the shadow detail in the original with a lot of finesse and control.

LAYER STYLES

In the same modal window as advanced blending options just noted, you'll find layer effects. The major layer styles in this dialog box use blend modes to accomplish its task, which makes them ripe for experimentation to see how Adobe uses them. It's also perfect for painting with blend modes to create special effects.

With the Blending window open, check out the classic Drop Shadow effect at the bottom of the layer styles selections on the left (**2.13**). The default blend mode is Multiply, you can choose the shadow color, and there's an opacity slider. You have everything you need to create some amazing effects. I don't have room to explain every detail about layer styles, but here are some of the highlights:

- Many effects rely on transparency, but not all of them apply to the same region. Drop shadows and outer glows apply outside the boundary of opaque pixels—that is, they extend into the transparent areas of the layer—while inner glow applies to the inside boundary.

- Each of the effects has controls for blending and opacity you can use in any combination.

- When used with the Fill option, you can isolate many layer styles.

- Some effects have contour options that control how the effect is distributed. Think of these as a variation on the boundary, but it's best at first to experiment with them rather than try to understand them. Once you have wrangled them a bit, you'll get the hang of each one's characteristics.

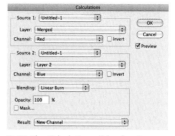

2.14 The Calculations dialog box has many options for blending channels from various layers.

Layer styles can be applied to layers with image content, or they can be used while painting to make adjustments and create new textures.

APPLY IMAGE AND CALCULATIONS

These two controls have a lot of power; and center on using blend modes for channels, selection, and masks. They are similar in that they combine elements using blend modes and return the result as a single output. Calculations is a channel blending tool, so it allows you to blend any two RGB, gray, or transparency channels from any given layer in the current document, and even combine the result with an existing mask. You can also use any open document that has the same bit depth, color space, and dimensions. The output can be a new alpha channel, selection, or even a new document (**2.14**).

While a full description of Calculations is beyond the scope of this book, you'll find several recipes that rely on this amazing tool. Check out the appendix for some great online references.

Apply Image is similar to Calculations, but has some significant differences. The biggest difference is that the output, as well as half of the input, is derived from the currently selected layer. It also writes directly to the currently active layer, replacing whatever was previously there. Keep this in mind before you overwrite your original image.

Input for Apply Image is the currently active layer and any other layer in the current or open documents. However, you can choose the composite RGB layer or individual channels. Calculations allows you to choose any two arbitrary channels and layers in the currently open documents.

SMART OBJECTS

One of the great things about blend modes is that they are non-destructive. You can change them at any time without losing image data. But once you've applied a filter to a layer, you are stuck with it. This is very limiting when you are experimenting with different ideas or fine-tuning an image.

While I do not always use the following method, many techniques can benefit from Smart Objects (SO). With a layer selected, open the Layers context menu by Alt+clicking (Windows) or Option+clicking (Mac) the layer you want to preserve, and choose "Convert to Smart Object." Alternatively, from the top menu, you could choose Layers > Smart Objects > Convert to Smart Object.

Smart Objects convert your layer contents to an embedded document, almost like archiving within the Photoshop file. This archived copy is displayed in the layer only as a reference, or virtual copy, of the original. It allows you to edit the layer contents in the PSD file without changing the archived layer contents. You can also apply most of the Filter menu items without changing the original layer.

While not all filters and effects are available when using SOs, most of them are, including the very valuable Blur and Distort filters. Many techniques described in this book make use of a blur, and some require the user to "eyeball" the results. If you accept the blur settings and later change your mind, you generally have to delete the layer (or undo the previous action) and start over. When your layer is a SO, you can easily adjust or remove the blur.

There's an even more powerful advantage to using SOs when you filter a layer: You get to change the blend mode of the filter! Typically, this is available only when using the Edit > Fade command (as noted previously.) In this case, the SO allows you to change the blend mode and opacity at any time, in addition to modifying the filter settings, themselves.

BUILDING REFERENCE IMAGES

You can experiment with color blending and other effects in many ways, but most people rely on tinkering with an image of interest. I prefer to abstract things a bit. To do this, I build example files that allow me to manipulate various settings and see their effects without the direct bias of the "attractiveness" of a given image.

The key with this method is to pay attention to the relationship between your manipulations and the results based on the colors and kinds of changes you are making. Although you can devise many additional files and scenarios, the best test is often done with an image you want to adjust. Keeping reference files at hand, or building them as the mood strikes, is a great way to acquire a better instinct for what you might want to do with a particular image.

For global color comparisons, I built the RGB triangles you see in the blend mode descriptions. This set of gray bars on each channel is rotated 120 degrees so each channel has equal representation in combination with the others, as well as a "pure" color. Each point of the triangle is white in only one channel, and then steps through a gradient to black at the opposite edge. The net result is that the centroid of the triangle should represent 50% gray, and everything moving away from that point shows a combination of the other colors. Along an edge, only two colors are mixed—those between the associated points (**2.15**).

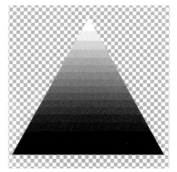

2.15 This triangle represents the gray values on a single channel. Other channels have the same triangle, but rotated to represent the spectrum of RGB colors. White represents 100% color and black represents 0% color.

NOTE The images in this book were converted to CMYK for print use. The original reference files were built in RGB, the typical working space for imaging professionals. In fact, all of the blend modes were programmed specifically for RGB, which is why many of them do not appear when working with CMYK images in Photoshop. You can download the files from my website (www. lightningsymphony.com) to see the RGB color images, which can appear dramatically different on the screen compared to the book.

NOTE A similar model can be built with CMYK, but Lab presents a unique challenge that is discussed in the appendices. The blend mode descriptions shows two squares with full spectra in both RGB and CMYK.

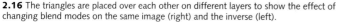

2.16 The triangles are placed over each other on different layers to show the effect of changing blend modes on the same image (right) and the inverse (left).

2.17 The gradient is sandwiched between the solid bars.

To compare blend modes, I placed two copies of the RGB triangle on one layer, and above that I duplicated the layer to retain the positioning (**2.16**). One of the triangles is inverted in color space to show how colors are blended with themselves and their RGB "opposites." Because most photographers and digital artists usually work in some flavor of RGB space, this color model is shown first.

Another experiment should be run on a single solid color over a full-spectrum gradient. The color bars show both stacking orders: solid on top of gradient, and then gradient on top of solid. Stacking order is important to a few recipes, especially when blending more than two layers. Again, this sample is built by addressing each channel independently (**2.17**).

Perhaps most dramatic among these example files is this continuous spectrum image showing the same gradient in a square configuration, duplicated and rotated 90 degrees. Because of the linearity, this example lets every color in the spectrum interact one time with every other color. Limits on display capabilities may make such images appear to have artifacts, but numerically the gradient is free from patterns. If you change the blend

2.18 Rotating a duplicate spectrum gives every color a chance to interact with every other color one time. Note the black line showing where a color is subtracted from itself.

mode to Difference, you will see a black line extend diagonally from one corner to another, which shows where the colors are the same because anything minus itself is zero, or black (**2.18**).

Building further on this spectrum example, you can add primary color bars in various orientations on a third layer. This is a great way to investigate the results of using one blend's output as input for another blend. This example also shows where layers used as translucent stacks begin to fail in terms of blend modes. Blend modes by themselves do not affect the opacity of a given pixel, just the color. Thus, the result of any blend becomes the direct input for the next higher blend. Adjusting opacity of the blended layers, of course, also has an effect, but I'll leave you to experiment with that.

Finally, a more targeted example is in order. You should use this when you want to dial in specific colors and opacities. It is a pretty simple file to build but is very useful for understanding

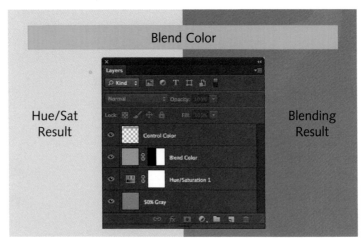

Blend Color

Hue/Sat
Result

Blending
Result

2.19 A reference file that lets you easily choose any solid color to investigate how each blend mode behaves with specific colors.

NOTE Each reference file is intended to help you visualize various blend combinations. I have provided them as downloads on my site (http://lightningsymphony.com/hpobm), and you are free to share them as long as you include attribution and a direct link. Please do not host them on your site, copy them, or provide them in any other downloads or media.

blend modes in a more discreet way. The bottom layer is a 50% gray fill with a Hue/Saturation adjustment layer clipped to it. With the Colorize button in the Hue/Saturation dialog box selected, you can change the color and saturation to pretty much anything in the RGB spectrum. The next layer above these two is filled with any solid color you wish to investigate and is the layer you will blend. Add a linear gradient from black to white in the mask so the underlying color shows through on one corner, and the fully opaque blend color appears in the other.

Add two bars in the mask, one white and one black, to see the solid base and blend colors next to the variations in opacity. And above all of this, create a single, solid bar of the blend color on a new layer that will not be blended as your color control point so you can track how much the blend color changes (**2.19**).

To use this example, fill the blend and control layers with the color you want to investigate. Then, use the Hue/Saturation adjustment layer to change the background. Of course, you can change the stacking order of these layers just as easily.

PART II
CREATIVE TECHNIQUES

Techniques in the following chapters cover photography, design, illustration, and special effects. From enhancements to whimsy, there's something for everyone here.

CHAPTER 3
PHOTOGRAPHY

The following techniques replicate traditional darkroom corrections, and are meant to be subtle enhancements rather than special effects. They take the place of filters, cutting frisket, and the dodge-and-burn shuffle.

Soft Light

Screen

Multiply

Just the Essentials

Photoshop includes more than two dozen blend modes in the Layers panel. For someone just starting out with the program (or even if you've used it for a while), the sheer number of blend modes can be daunting. Even worse, scrolling through the list trying to find the right one is time consuming. After looking at my own workflow and studying the techniques of many other pros out there, I've realized you'll really use only four blend modes most of the time. So you don't need to worry about the rest, at least for a while.

- **Multiply** is a darkening blend mode that darkens while appearing to deepen some of the colors (especially reds, blues, and greens).

- **Screen**, the exact opposite of Multiply, brightens your photos and can almost make them look washed out in some cases.

- **Overlay** and **Soft Light** are contrast-enhancing blend modes that work similarly, rendering the dark parts of an image darker and the bright parts brighter while making the colors pop a little more.

  The difference between the two is that Overlay is more intense than Soft Light and typically has a more punchy quality. That punch sometimes looks just great and does the trick. At other times, however, Overlay can make colors look oversaturated.

  When that happens, try Soft Light. It's a subdued version of Overlay that does a fantastic job giving your image a little contrast boost without making it look radioactive.

So, the next time you're looking at that huge blend mode list and wondering where to start, first try one of these four modes. You'll be surprised at how many times one of them will be just perfect.

MATT KLOSKOWSKI
MATTKLOSKOWSKI.COM

1 Duplicate the background layer.
2 Apply Average Blur (Filter > Blur > Average Blur).
3 Invert the blurred layer.
4 Set the blurred layer to Color blend mode.
5 Reduce Opacity of the blend layer.

This is a quick way to remove an overall color cast when the cast is fairly strong and somewhat uniform, as when shooting through a colored gel. You'll typically find this kind of color cast in underwater or aquarium images, photos taken indoors under artificial lighting, or when the camera's white balance was set improperly. While most raw image processors can handle this directly, you can use this recipe for pictures taken with smaller cameras and mobile phones.

Duplicate the image layer, and change the name to *Color Cast*.

Choose Filter > Blur > Average to apply Average Blur to the Color Cast layer, which will fill the layer with the dominant color in the image.

Invert Color Cast by pressing Ctrl+I (Windows) or Command+I (Mac). This is the equivalent of placing a gel filter over your camera lens when taking the shot.

Change the blend mode on the Color Cast layer to Color, and lower the Opacity until you have neutralized the overall cast. Use the result as a base for additional corrections or effects. Using Hue instead of Color produces slightly more contrast for some images, as it applies preferentially to saturation rather than gray level brightness. ■

A great trick to quickly enhance a portrait is to lighten the eyes. Typically, this is done when the shot is captured, but sometimes a little post processing is called for. This technique is really, really quick.

On the background layer, use the Elliptical Marquee tool to select the eyes individually. After you've selected one eye, Shift-drag the second selection to get both eyes at the same time.

Press Ctrl+J (Windows) or Command+J (Mac) to copy the selection to a new layer. Apply a Gaussian blur (Filter > Blur > Gaussian) large enough to remove details while retaining general areas of color.

Change the blend mode of the duplicated layer to Overlay or Soft Light for more drama, or choose Screen with lower opacity to brighten them. You can also use Multiply to create a more illustrated, darker look.

You can further adjust the effect by painting in some highlights on another blank layer set to Soft Light mode. Using a large soft brush, paint with white just over the center of the eyes. You can usually get away with a single dab of pixels if your brush is slightly larger than the subject's eyes.

Then, lower opacity to about 30% to retain just a touch of highlight. ■

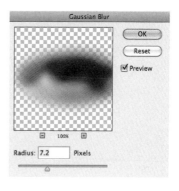

1 Create a blank layer above the base image.
2 Set the blank layer's blend mode to Overlay.
3 Paint with white to dodge, and black to burn. Shades of gray offer more subtle control.
4 Use a low-opacity brush and the Smudge tool for refinement.

One of the most common retouching techniques is to dodge and burn—selectively darkening or brightening areas of an image to locally increase contrast or enhance tone. This technique is not global, but is intended to apply changes very specifically. Here are two variations on this essential method of fine-tuning your photographs.

The first method is pretty straightforward. Create a new layer above the background and fill it with 50% gray. Set the gray layer's blend mode to Overlay. Now, you can use the Dodge and Burn tools directly on this layer. For the most precise control, you may want to use a digital tablet and pen.

While you can apply dodge and burn directly to the image, doing so is a destructive process. Using a gray layer enables the same level of control without changing the original image data. It is thereby quite easy to later correct mistakes or change the overall effect as needed.

The second method provides additional speed and a lot more flexibility. Instead of filling the Overlay layer with gray, simply paint on the empty layer with a brush set to Normal mode. Painting with black will darken the image (burn), and painting with white will lighten it (dodge); but you can also choose any color you wish. This technique requires more familiarity with the ways colors interact, so be sure to check the Overlay entry in the reference section of this book.

Start with a low Opacity brush, around 10%, and build to brighter or darker areas by degrees. A good practice is to keep the Swatches panel open and select gray levels directly.

Using these methods, you can erase, blur, or smudge the Overlay layer to refine and fix details in your corrections without altering the original image pixels at all. Win! ∎

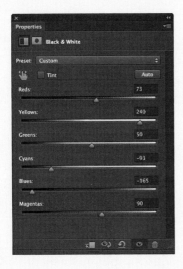

Like most people, I was always afraid of the blend modes near the bottom of the list. We all learn how to play with the common blending modes, such as Multiple/Screen, Color Dodge/ Burn, Overlay, and Soft Light. But when I started out, I asked multiple Photoshoppers out there, "What is Difference used for?" or "When do *you* use Luminosity?"

I rarely got an answer, and when I did, it went something like, "Oh, I'll try those sometimes just to explore what they might look like, but basically you'll never use them." However, you can realize some great results from these mysteriously shunned controls, and I'd like to share my favorite with you.

Starting with a photo that is muted but has even exposure, add a Black & White adjustment layer above it. You are looking only at the overall tone at this point, which is completely subjective. But this is the launch point for the next step.

Now, change the adjustment layer's blend mode to Luminosity.

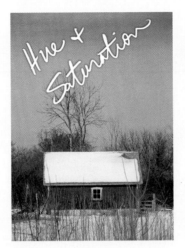
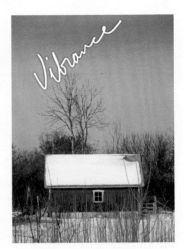

When I get stock photos, this is often my first step toward adjusting an image for better balance between colors in an exposure. I use this Luminosity trick to coax areas with little detail to have more information that I can enhance with Hue and Saturation set to Color—and can then target those specific colors again. Adding a Vibrance adjustment can make it all feel similar in the level of color intensity.

For an added bonus, you can also use this technique to creatively explore possibilities. Return to your Black & White adjustment layers presets, and instead of using Lighter, try applying Infrared, Blue, or High-Contrast Red as a setting. You may get some dramatic shifts in how your image looks, but don't be scared. You might like it.

MARK HEAPS
MARKHEAPS.COM

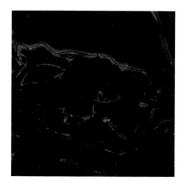

Sometimes an image doesn't need sharpening so much as additional edge contrast. The difference is really one of scale because sharpening tends to work on smaller features and details in the image. Edge contrast tends to spread out more and work on larger areas.

Duplicate your image layer, and then choose Filter > Blur > Gaussian Blur to blur most of the details. For this image, the long dimension is about 3500 pixels, and a setting of 22 px works well.

Set the blurred layer's blend mode to Difference. You should now have a mostly black canvas with only some of the higher contrast edges showing.

Stamp/Merge Visible using Ctrl+Shift+Alt+E (Windows) or Command+Shift+Option+E (Mac) to create a copy of your work.

Invert the merged copy (Ctrl+I on Windows, or Command+I on Mac) and set that layer's blend mode to Divide. The edges of high and moderate contrast regions are brightened, but not sharpened. You can also mix this technique with the High Pass sharpening techniques.

Finish with a Hue/Saturation adjustment layer to control saturation and possible color shift.

You can tune this effect to some extent by varying the amount of blur and opacity. ■

1 Duplicate the background layer.
2 Apply a large Gaussian blur.
3 Set the duplicate layer blend mode to Difference.
4 Stamp/Merge Visible.
5 Turn *off* the visibility of the blurred layer.
6 Invert the merged copy, and set the blend mode to Divide.
7 Add a Hue/Saturation layer, if necessary.

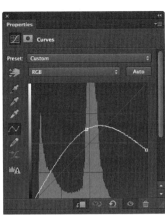

This is a great fix for slightly underexposed images taken on overcast days. It recovers highlights and increases contrast, and tends to introduce some color shift.

It's important to select an image that does not have any blown-out highlights because these will be emphasized. And large regions of black or very dark shadows can become muddy, which you'll learn how to fix.

Above your background layer, add a Curves adjustment layer, but don't change anything. Set the blend mode to Linear Dodge (Add) to brighten the image. Above that, add another Curves adjustment layer, and set its blend mode to Color Burn. Now, the secret is to clip the top layer to the middle layer. Alt-click (Windows) or Option-click (Mac) between the two layers to clip them.

This will appear to blow out the highlights quite a bit, but check out the curve screenshot. Lowering the whites and increasing the mids will give you more clarity and preserve the drama.

To recover muddy blacks and shadows, double-click the top Curves layer and adjust the Blend If sliders. Be sure to hold down Alt or Option to split the Blacks slider of the underlying layer as described in the General Techniques section. ■

While I normally advocate using Camera Raw to remove vignettes, the following method is a pretty handy way to realize some basic recovery using the Divide blend mode. It also leaves you some creative latitude for additional effects, but it does have some limitations.

Use the Eyedropper tool (I) to sample the dark corners of your image. I recommend using a larger sampling area, so set your range to an 11 x 11 sample in the Tool options. You want to sample the general color and darkness rather than a point sample. Clicking in the corner will load your foreground with that color.

Press X to swap the foreground and background colors, and then click in the central, brightest area of your image to identify the foundation colors you'll need.

Create a blank layer above your background, and choose the Gradient tool (G) with a radial gradient, using the Foreground to Background gradient in the upper left. (Click the Gradient sample drop-down menu on the options bar.) The bright foreground color should be in the center, and the background color should be at the outside of the gradient.

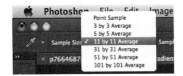

1. Use the Eyedropper tool to select the bright middle area as the foreground, and a dark corner as the background.

2. Create a radial gradient on a blank layer above the background layer.

3. Set the gradient layer's blend mode to Divide.

4. Lower opacity, apply a mask, and use Blend If as needed to control the effect.

On the blank layer, drag from the center of the canvas out to the corner. You should have a smooth gradient extended from the middle. Then, set the gradient layer blend mode to Divide. The effect will be immediate, if a bit harsh.

Lower the opacity of the Divide layer, and use Blend If to recover some of the highlight detail. In the sample image, Blend If was applied to the gradient layer, moving the white sliders on This Layer from right to left, and splitting them quite a bit to soften the transition.

This technique can be faster than Camera Raw on some simple images, and allows you to change the center of the vignette correction much more easily. Plus, you have the added ability to adjust the colors or add a refinement mask, something Camera Raw does not offer.

Unfortunately, this technique doesn't work as well with complex images or images with dark centers. You'll have to mask those manually. On the other hand, this is a great way to remove backgrounds that are flat but unevenly lit.

Bonus! If you are able to first shoot a "flat field" image with no subject, you'll have the source for your Divide blend mode layer. Simply replace the gradient with your subject-free background. ■

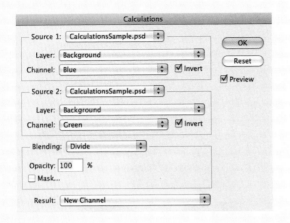

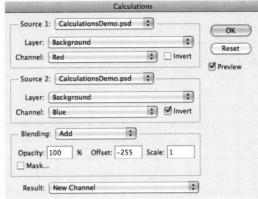

An often overlooked use of blend modes is Calculations. The Calculations tool relies entirely on combining channels using blend mode operations and provides an amazing amount of power for retouchers.

Here is a small breakdown of some of the combinations that I find helpful for generating masks nearly automatically. These methods use data already in the image, which minimizes your work.

To use these, save your results as a new channel, and then name the new channel in the Channels panel. When you need to adjust target areas, choose Select > Load Selection and choose the saved selection channel you want. You can use the active selection to copy from the background to a new layer, fill on a new layer, or create an adjustment layer using the selection as a mask.

These listings identify the channel selections in order, the blend mode, and any additional settings that go with the blend mode. For this example, all selections were made from the background image with no other layers visible:

- **Select shadows:** Gray (inverted), Gray (inverted), Color Burn or Linear Burn, 100% opacity. Adjusting the opacity affects the smoothness of the mask.

- **Select light skin:** Red, Blue (inverted) or Green (inverted), Add, –255, 1

- **Select yellow-dominated areas:** Gray, Blue, Divide, 100% opacity
- **Select red-dominated areas:** Gray, Green, Divide, 100% opacity
- **Select greens, blues (varies):** Green, Red, Divide, 100% opacity
- **Select pink/magenta areas:** Blue, Green, Divide, 100% opacity
- **Select yellow heavy areas:** Green (inverted), Blue (inverted), Subtract, 0, 1
- **Select red heavy areas:** Red (inverted), Blue (inverted), Subtract, 0, 1

All of these settings use the Layer pop-up set to Merged. This uses whatever is currently visible, though it is possible to use any single active layer, or even another open document that is the same size, bit depth, and color mode. As an added bonus, you can even use the newly created channel as one of the inputs to further refine the results.

These settings just touch upon what can be done using calculations and different blend modes. While they can be used for targeted photographic corrections, it's also possible to apply the results in more creative ways, such as custom posterization.

CHRIS TARANTINO
CHRISTARANTINO.COM

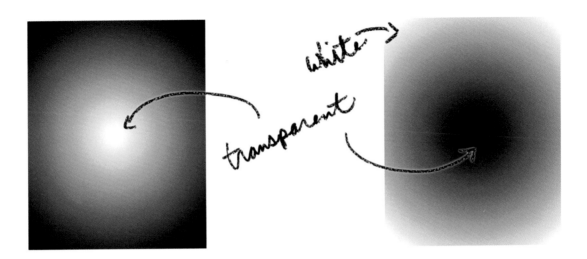

While another technique showed you how to remove unwanted vignetting, you'll find that putting it back in is actually a bit easier. As a creative effect, vignetting has many variations, and here are some of my favorites.

All of these vignettes start with some kind of border on a layer above your background image. You can create that border using a solid fill with the central region deleted or masked, or you can paint it. You can even use your background image or other elements, such as scrollwork.

In the top example, I used a solid black brush with very soft edges on a blank layer. After painting the areas I wanted to darken with black, I set the blend mode to Overlay. This achieved a traditional look, simulating a familiar kind of vignetting.

The middle example was created by duplicating the background layer and setting the duplicate's mode to Hard Mix. A mask was applied to bring back the original image in the center. Finally, the Fill value of the duplicate was lowered to about 80%.

You can also create a vignette by lightening the edges of the image. The bottom right example is the same as the top image, but I painted with white instead of black. You could combine this with Sepia and Soft Glow techniques to produce an aged, antique photo look. ∎

A handful of techniques in this book deal with adjusting luminosity. While each technique can have similar results, the degree of control and type of interaction varies greatly. And each technique has unique variations.

This one was described to me by Rocky Berlier, who happens to be the technical editor for this book. Loosely based on the Ansel Adams 10-Zone System, it gives you parametric control over multiple luminosity regions.

Add a Gradient Map adjustment layer over the background layer, and set the adjustment layer's blend mode to Luminosity.

Press D to load the default black-and-white colors for foreground and background. Double-click the adjustment layer's thumbnail to open it, and choose the black-and-white gradient. At the bottom of the dialog box, you'll see a representation of the gradient. Clicking below the bar lets you set a color stop. Add three stops near the 25%, 50%, and 75% positions.

Double-click each of these in turn, and set the B value of the HSB section to the values I've previously listed. This sets the brightness value, which is effectively the gray level for each color stop when Hue and Saturation are set to zero (black). When the brightness value lines up with the position (as read in the Location box), the effect is neutral, that is, no changes

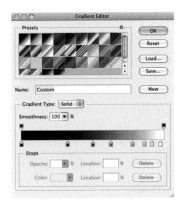

are made to the image. Dragging a slider to the left of neutral brightens that zone, apparently increasing exposure. Dragging to the right decreases exposure and darkens the zone.

Adding more sliders gives you finer control, but be aware that the brightness value you enter should be the middle value between its neighbors. So, if you need a value between 25% and 50% to realize more control in the middle dark tones, start with around 37%. Of course, you can deviate from this general guideline as you get a better feel for how the technique works with a particular image.

Saving these various settings to build a good collection of gradients with different numbers of sliders and colors will serve you well with this technique. ■

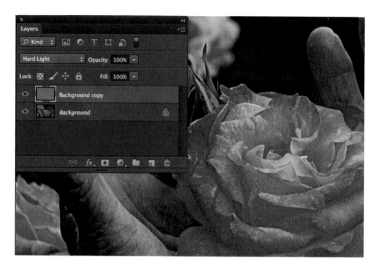

1 Duplicate the background layer and convert it to a Smart Object.

2 Set the duplicate layer's blend mode to Hard Light.

3 Apply the High Pass filter (Filter > Other > High Pass) at 3% to 5% of the long pixel dimension.

Adobe Photoshop, and some plug-ins, include good tools for sharpening images. However, by using a manual method, you can see the sharpening results in real time and make additional adjustments.

Duplicate the background layer, and name the duplicate *Sharpen*. Convert this layer to a Smart Object (Filter > Convert for Smart Filters). Set the Sharpen layer's blend mode to Hard Light, and choose Filter > Other > High Pass to apply the High Pass filter. Adjust the Radius slider according to your tastes. You can see the sharpening effect immediately. By using the Smart Object method, you can adjust the sharpening effect later on.

Setting the blend mode first allows you to see the effect while adjusting the High Pass filter. After you've added an acceptable amount of sharpening, you can adjust the effect in several ways. First, try lowering the opacity. If you want to apply different effects to the highlights, you can also set other blend modes such as Soft Light, Linear Light, or Vivid Light.

You can optionally add a Hue/Saturation adjustment layer to control color shift.

Finally, try using luminosity blending (Blend If under Advanced Blending on the layer options). (See the General Techniques section for details.) Doing so will let you selectively apply the effect based on brightness values. ■

Similar to the High Pass Sharpening 1 method, this technique uses High Pass. However, it adds a brightness adjustment by folding in the Screen blend mode. By using Smart Objects, you can save a couple of steps when you need to make additional changes to contrast or brightness. In this specific example, you'll increase brightness and add a little contrast to the image.

Duplicate the background layer, and convert to a Smart Object (Filter > Convert for Smart Filters). Then apply the High Pass filter.

Next, double-click the small icon on the High Pass filter entry in the Layers panel, and choose Linear Light. Leave the Opacity slider at 100%.

Finally, change the blend mode of the Smart Object layer to Screen, and lower the layer's opacity to 80%.

You could use other blend modes in the same group depending on the situation. One of the challenges when using this method is that you can't refine the amount of sharpening while watching the effect. The secret sauce is to pay careful attention to the High Pass filter's halo effects and use a little less of the filter than you think you should. A rule of thumb is to set the filter's input slider at around 5% of the longest pixel dimension. ■

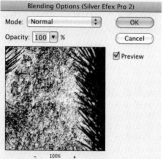

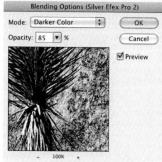

Blend modes allow me to work with finesse, speed, and power; and I am always surprised by how useful and flexible they are. I use them consistently when I'm retouching and compositing; but one of my favorite times to issue them is when I'm exploring the digital darkroom to enhance a single image to best portray my vision. To maintain creative flexibility, I use Smart Filters, which have the added value of opacity and Blend Mode controls. (Choose Filter > Convert for Smart Filters.)

Using Nik Silver Efex Pro 2, I convert the color image to black and white, which in this example created a very strong effect that I wanted to make more subtle.

To access the blend modes of the Smart Filters, double-click the small triangle control, and change Mode to Darker Color. Then, reduce the Opacity to 85% to allow some of the color to shimmer though while maintaining density.

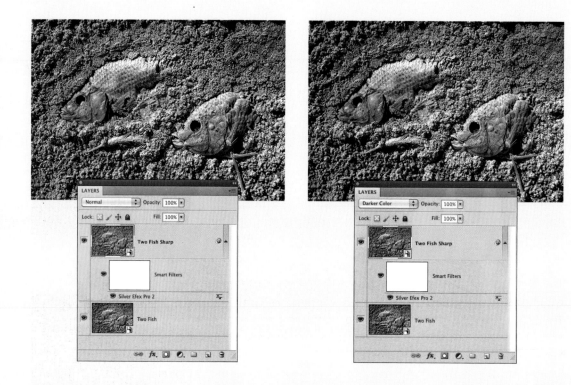

Now I take advantage of blend modes to apply subtle sharpening. Start again by making your layer a Smart Object (choose Filter > Convert for Smart Filters), and then make a copy by choosing Layer > Smart Objects > New Smart Objects via Copy.

I used Nik Silver Efex Pro 2 to add a highly structured sharpening to enhance the prehistoric feel of the Salton Sea fish. By changing the layer blend mode to Darker Color, the contrast was reduced and the shadows were given a greater depth.

The most important aspect of working with blend modes is to experiment and play. Often there is no right or wrong way—just try it!

KATRIN EISMANN
KATRINEISMANN.COM

Curves adjustments are fantastic for performing overall corrections or generally changing an image. However, they alter both brightness/luminosity as well as saturation, elements you sometimes need to control individually.

To do so, simply add two Curves adjustment layers. Set the bottom layer to Luminosity blend mode, and the top layer to Saturation.

You can also control each of these Curves adjustments on individual channels by using the dialog box's Channel menu. So, you get three channels of flexibility for both Luminosity and Saturation. And of course, you can also use the layer's individual masks.

This same technique can be used for selective color corrections by changing the blend mode to Hue or Color. And for more extreme adjustments, consider using Multiply or Hard Light instead of Luminosity. ■

CHAPTER 4
PHOTOGRAPHIC MANIPULATION & COMPOSITING

These techniques are aimed at creative interpretations and special effects. They tend to be a little more extreme, and many recipes can be combined quite easily.

Blend modes are a great way to add texture and color to your compositions. They are very easy to experiment with, letting you explore all kinds of options. For my image, Ephemeral, I combined the following modes to achieve a subtle, balanced, mysterious feeling:

- Soft Light—Lower contrast than Overlay, and used for the ripples

- Overlay—Applied to the mountain reflection for contrast, but with low opacity and a slight blur

- Hard Light—A gradient layer to add color to the ice and mountains

- Normal—Applied to the pebbles at low opacity

I usually know what I want each layer to add to my final image, but sometimes I like to wander through the blend modes before making up my mind, which can provide some wonderfully unexpected results. You can easily do this by moving through each blend mode in turn. With the Move tool selected (V), press Shift++ (plus) or Shift+− (minus) to scroll through the modes.

Overlay and Soft Light blend my images together without dominating, while lowering opacity alone was enough to keep some interesting texture from the pebbles. Hard Light provided just the right splash of color. It was important that the elements not fight for attention, but build in harmony and lead the eye.

JULIEANNE KOST
JKOST.COM

Here is a tip for adding some pop to portraits, originally given to me by Matt Kloskowski: Add a self-blend overlay. That's it. Duplicating the base image and setting its mode to Overlay is a great way to add contrast and saturation to evenly lit portraits.

However, you can include a lot of control by blurring the duplicate and adding a Hue/Saturation adjustment layer. Doing so gives you the flexibility to dial in several different looks quite easily. For the example image, I used Filter > Blur > Gaussian Blur at about 20 pixels on the duplicate layer.

After setting the blurred duplicate to Overlay blend mode, I used a Hue/Saturation adjustment layer clipped to the duplicate. Alt-click (Windows) or Option-click (Mac) between the duplicate and adjustment layers when the cursor changes to a downward-pointing arrow and a box. (In Photoshop CS5.5 and earlier, this icon was a double ring.)

Double-click the adjustment layer to open it, and select the Colorize option. Now you can move the sliders to get the precise look you want. Lower the opacity of either the duplicate or the adjustment layer, if necessary.

Power users will want to take advantage of converting the duplicate to a Smart Object before blurring, and also use the Blend If sliders on the adjustment layer's advanced blending dialog box. Be aware that making this adjustment on the Hue/Saturation layer is different from doing so on the duplicate. ■

1 Duplicate the background layer.

2 Convert the duplicate to a Smart Object.

3 Apply Gaussian blur to the duplicate (as a Smart Filter).

4 Change the blend mode of the duplicate to Overlay.

5 Add a clipped Hue/Saturation adjustment layer to the duplicate.

6 Use the Colorize option in the adjustment layer.

1 Fill a new layer above your background image with 50% gray.

2 Change the blend mode to Color or Hue.

3 Add a Hue/Saturation adjustment layer above the gray layer, and clip it. (See the Introduction section for details on this technique.) Set the Hue and Saturation sliders to 40, leaving Lightness at 0.

4 In the adjustment layer, select the Colorize option.

It's very easy to achieve a retro look with an image by adding a color or tone. A common way to do this is to create a blank layer above the background image, fill that layer with the color of your choice, and set the blend mode to Color. Everything brighter than black will take the new color according to its luminosity, as if the image were first converted to grayscale.

To take this idea further, try using Hue instead. This mode will pay more attention to the saturation in the original image, being less strongly applied where saturation is low, as in neutral or pastel colors.

For serious power or when you don't know which color you want, fill the blend layer with 50% gray, and then add a clipped Hue/Saturation adjustment layer. Here's where the difference between Hue and Color blend modes really stands out. When the gray layer is set to Hue, the Saturation slider has no effect until you drag it all the way to the left. That's because Hue ignores the blend layer saturation and, instead, uses the saturation of the base. Color, on the other hand, applies both the Saturation and the Hue of the blend layer, so both controls work.

Color is great for making an image more monochrome, so it's best used when you want a definite and obvious tint. Hue is a better choice for realizing subtle changes and drama. ∎

A variation on applying sepia or other colors to an image is to apply a hand-tinted look to photographs by painting color only where you want it, and leaving the rest of the photo in grayscale.

If necessary, apply a Black & White adjustment layer over the background image and fine-tune it as you like. The advantage of using the adjustment layer is that you can later modify the relative contrast between hues precisely, and lower the opacity to recover some of the original color.

Create a blank layer above the adjustment layer, and set the blend mode to Color.

Using the Brush tool (B) on the blank layer, fill in the areas you want with the color of your choice. You can combine multiple colors on a single layer, but remember that any overlap will show only the current color. If you run into a previous paint stroke, you'll have to reselect that color to remove any blemishes or overlaps.

This technique is especially nice when used with less saturated colors, and the overall opacity is lowered a bit. You can optionally change the Black & White adjustment layer's blending to Saturation for less overall contrast, and also lower its opacity.

The example image uses the B&W adjustment set to Hue blend mode, with 90% opacity to smooth out the tones and allow just a little of the base color to show through. ∎

1 Add a Black & White adjustment layer above Background.

2 Change the adjustment layer blend mode to Hue.

3 Create a blank layer above adjustment layer.

4 Set the blank layer to Color blend mode.

5 Paint on a blank layer to fill in color.

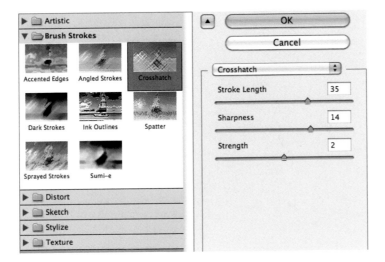

Want a quick color sketch? This recipe serves as a foundation for several other looks. You can control the width of the lines by varying the amount of blur; and you can apply other kinds of blur or even distortions. As long as the Divide blend mode has something other than itself to compare with, you'll get visible results.

Start by duplicating the background layer, and set the blend mode of the duplicate to Divide.

Next, apply a blur. To get a feel for this look, start with Gaussian blur (choose Filter > Blur > Gaussian Blur) at about 10 pixels. The dialog box will display a real-time preview of the results, which allows you to experiment and dial-in the effect.

That's pretty much the entire recipe. But you can use it to kick off all kinds of variations. For example, in the facing image I used "the claw"—press Ctrl+Alt+Shift+E (Windows) or Command+Option+Shift+E (Mac)—to copy/merge visible to a new layer. This captured the drawing look, so I could apply a Crosshatch filter by choosing Filter > Filter Gallery > Crosshatch. Finally, the blend mode was set to Linear Burn. ■

1 Duplicate the background layer.

2 Set the duplicate's blend mode to Divide.

3 Apply a small Gaussian blur to the duplicate.

4 Optionally copy/merge to a new layer, and apply additional filters. Set the filtered layer to Linear Burn.

final effect

inverted copy

The previous sketch technique creates a unique look. This variation produces thinner lines, which looks more like a traditional line sketch. However, the secret sauce here is Smart Objects.

Duplicate the background image layer by pressing Ctrl+J (Windows) or Command+J (Mac). Invert the duplicate by pressing Ctrl/Command+I. Convert it to a Smart Object by right-clicking or Control-clicking (Mac) the layer in the panel, and choosing Convert to Smart Object. Now you can experiment with virtually any of the filters available in Photoshop.

Before applying a filter, though, change the blend mode of the Smart Object to Linear Dodge (Add). The result should be solid white. With the layer selected, choose Filter > Brush Strokes > Crosshatch. In the Filter Gallery, choose low settings—Stroke Length 12, Sharpness 6, Strength 2—as starting points.

Keep in mind that the preview will show only the effect applied to the image layer, and not display the image layer blended with the background. Click OK to apply the settings, and check out the results. This effect works best with images that have good to strong contrast and clear edges. Color is not as important to the final effect, but various levels of brightness really do make a difference.

Use the Smart Filters to try various settings and filters to dial in just the right look. ■

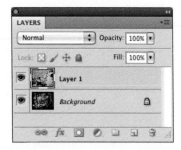

The Divide blend mode is a recent entry to Photoshop, and has become one of those blend modes I love to use to weather an image and add a bit of texture.

Start with a black-and-white image that you want to give a cool texture. Open a second image that you will use as a texture. Select the Move tool, and drag the second image to the original image. For this image, I chose to transform the pattern to fit into the image and desaturate it (Image > Adjustments > Desaturate).

The Divide blend mode works well with strong, saturated colors, so I use an adjustment layer of Levels to drag in my shadow and highlights a little bit. When that's complete, I can merge the adjustment layer and the textured layer together.

Now that this texture is ready, switch your blend mode to Divide. If your image doesn't look like it changed, don't worry. Press Ctrl+I (Windows) or Command+I (Mac) to invert the texture. The Divide blend mode uses white colors to screen the image below. The black portions of the image are treated as white splotches on the image to create a textured look.

At this point, you could apply a layer mask and remove the effect from the portion of the image you want to keep clean. This method is a great way to give a good picture a textured look.

RC CONCEPCION
ABOUTRC.COM

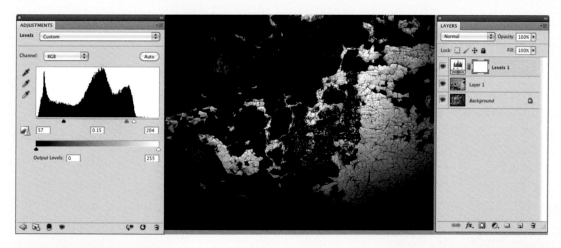

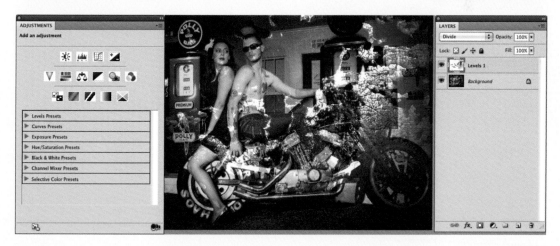

In the days of slide film, Michael Orton created a signature effect that involved stacking two or three transparencies to create a dreamy, soft effect. This effect was traditionally achieved by shooting identical compositions with different levels of focus. The out-of-focus images contributed the softness, while the sharp image provided the details.

In the digital realm, you can closely recreate that effect with some simple techniques. However, refining the effect can take quite a bit of finesse.

Start by duplicating the background layer. The duplicate is given a large Gaussian blur to remove detail and leave only large, soft blobs of color. This sometimes reduces the apparent saturation, so you should consider adding a clipped Hue/Saturation adjustment layer. Set this layer to Multiply blend mode, but lower the Opacity to around 30%.

Duplicate the blurred layer and desaturate it. Press Ctrl+U (Windows) or Command+U (Mac) to open the Hue/Saturation dialog box, and drag the Saturation slider all the way to the left. Set this layer to Screen blend mode to provide the bright glow. Lower Opacity to around 70%. Screen mode can cause some of the darks beneath the layer to become soft or muddy, so open the Advanced Blending dialog box and drag the Underlying Layer dark sliders to return some of the shadow detail. ∎

1   Duplicate the background layer, and apply a large Gaussian blur (10% of the long side pixel dimensions).

2   Set the duplicate to Multiply blend mode, and lower Opacity to 30%.

3   Duplicate that altered layer.

4   Desaturate the new duplicate, and set it to Screen blend mode at 70% Opacity.

5   Optionally include a Hue/Saturation adjustment layer to the Multiply layer to increase saturation.

6   Optionally adjust the Blend If sliders on the Screen layer to recover shadow detail.

1 Open the Advanced Blending dialog box.

2 Adjust the This Layer Blend If sliders.

3 Create a blank layer above the adjusted layer.

4 Shift-click to select both the blank and adjusted layers.

5 Press Ctrl/Command+E to merge the layers.

Other techniques in this book show you how to selectively blend layers using the Advanced Blend If sliders, thereby allowing some of the base image to show through the blend image. But what if you want to apply layer effects to the opaque areas? Applying a layer style such as Drop Shadow or Bevel & Emboss has no effect, except at the edges of the layer content.

You can trap the transparency with this neat trick, which can save lots of time compared to traditional masking methods.

Add a blending layer with some high-contrast texture above your base. The current example uses an image of leaves over a plain, white background layer.

Open the Advanced Blending dialog box, and adjust the sliders for This Layer to allow the bottom layer to show through. Keep in mind that effects such as Drop Shadow work best on edges next to totally transparent areas.

Create a blank layer above the duplicate, and Shift-click the duplicate to select both layers. Press Ctrl+E (Windows) or Command+E (Mac) to merge the layers and trap the transparency of the blend layer just as if you had created a mask and applied it to the layer. ∎

Sometimes an image needs to have just a little noise for texture, but controlling the effect can be a tedious process when using Filter > Noise > Add Noise. This very quick method gives you tons of flexibility and control: Use adjustment layers set to Dissolve.

Above your image layer, add an adjustment layer (Brightness and Contrast, Curves, Exposure, or Black & White are good candidates) and lower the opacity to 50%. Set the adjustment layer's blend mode to Dissolve, and start tweaking the controls. Different adjustment layers produce a variety of effects and allow you to control where and how noise appears in the image.

Start by adjusting Brightness and Contrast, Curves, or Exposure to add basic noise that you can independently control in shadows and highlights. For a more drastic look, use Black & White, which usually needs some additional filtering to make it look good (or use it with graphic design elements).

Because the Dissolve mode can appear very harsh, small adjustments are probably all you will need. In many cases, the noise is just a starting point, so try duplicating the background layer and merging the adjustment layer with the copy. Then, apply a blur and additional blend modes for variety. ■

Tons of graphic novel and illustration effects are quite easy to create. This first method is very quick, and works well with nicely saturated images and images with lots of dynamic range.

Duplicate the background layer, and set the blending mode to Divide. Next, choose Filter > Blur > Gaussian Blur to blur the duplicate. Start with a small blur, about 9 to 10 px for a 4000 px image. You can see the effect change as you adjust the slider.

Make another duplicate of the blurred layer, and apply the same blur. This time, change the blend mode to Linear Burn.

You can get a softer look by using Multiply on the top layer, which is good for images with less dynamic range or detail, and those with a definite overall color tone. ■

1   Duplicate the background layer.
2   Blur the duplicate and set it to Divide blend mode.
3   Duplicate the blurred layer.
4   Apply another blur to the top layer and change it to Linear Burn.

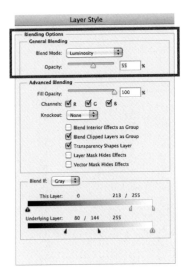

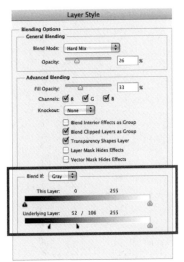

You can create a look that is closer to Orton's deep saturation using a variant of the Soft Glow 1 technique.

Follow the steps for Soft Glow 1, then make the following changes. Set the first blurred duplicate to Normal (instead of Multiply) to retain more of the original color. The Hue/Saturation layer does not change.

Set the desaturated, blurred layer to Luminosity (instead of Screen), but lower Opacity to 55%. Duplicate this layer and set it to Hard Mix. Reduce Fill to 33% and Opacity to 26% for this image. Treat both of the desaturated layers to some Blend If Luminosity adjustments to produce smoother color transitions.

The end result is more saturated and vibrant, lending an even more surreal—if less peaceful—look.

Base images that have specular highlights near fields of color—such as surface reflections from a deep green or blue body of water—will benefit most from this treatment. It is easy to lose definition with this effect, so pay attention to darks, which should be mostly left alone. ∎

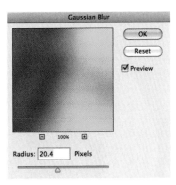

This effect adds some pixelated noise around the high-contrast edges in an image. For flexibility, it uses Smart Objects, which allow the effect to be fine-tuned.

Duplicate the background layer and convert it to a Smart Object—right-click the layer and choose Convert to Smart Object. Next, from the Channels panel, choose a channel with good midrange values. Drag that channel to the Create New Channel icon to duplicate it.

For this example image, the green channel worked well after a little adjustment to Levels (press Ctrl/Command+M) to bring up the highlights.

In the Smart Object layer, load the channel selection (from the Channel pop-up menu, choose Select > Load Selection > Green Copy), and then click the Add Layer Mask button to convert the selection to a mask.

With the Smart Object layer still selected, change its blend mode to Dissolve. Finally, choose Filter > Blur > Gaussian Blur, and adjust the slider. This sunflower needed about 20 pixels, based on its size and resolution.

The mask confines the amount of noise from the Dissolve blend mode to bright areas. As the mask gets darker, there is less noise, so the effect is less pronounced. ■

1 Duplicate the background layer.
2 Convert the duplicate to a Smart Object.
3 Duplicate a contrasty channel to use as a mask.
4 Load the selection as a mask on the Smart Object.
5 Change the Smart Object's blend mode to Dissolve.
6 Add Gaussian blur to the Smart Object to show pixilated edges.

You can use the difference between Opacity and Fill to alter the effect of some blend modes. To make a custom lens flair/glow effect, choose an appropriate beauty or landscape shot, and create an empty layer by clicking the Create New Layer icon near the bottom of the Layers panel.

Press D to reset your foreground color to black and the background color to white. Choose a large, soft brush about the size of the glow you want to create. On the blank layer, first paint with black in one spot until you have a big, black, soft-edged circle. Press X to swap the foreground and background colors, and then paint with white on top of the circle.

Change the blend mode of the layer to Color Dodge. When you lower the opacity using the Opacity slider, the effect becomes dull and unattractive. However, when you lower the opacity using the Fill slider, Photoshop makes the appropriate blend to keep the Color Dodge effect pronounced. See the Layers panel screenshot for details on the values to use.

You can further refine this look by choosing the Smudge tool and pushing the highlights around as in the current image. If you need to see your work more clearly, return the layer's blend mode to Normal and return the Fill values to 100%.

CARRIE BEENE
CARRIENYC.COM

1   Duplicate the background layer.
2   Blur the copy with Gaussian blur to about 0.5% to 1.0% of the long pixel dimension.
3   Set the blend mode of the copy to Hard Mix.
4   Reduce the Fill to between 20% and 70%.
5   Reduce the Opacity.
6   Adjust the Blend If sliders.

You can use this method to increase contrast and saturation in otherwise dull images. However, it can quite easily blow out highlights, and darker images will tend to oversaturate in some areas.

As you adjust the settings, pay attention to the highlights and shadows, but don't be afraid to push them into clipping (solid black or white). You can ease the impact on these areas by using Blend If on the layer adjustments to restore detail. (See General Techniques for more details.)

Duplicate your background layer and give it a slight blur, just enough to smooth out hard edges. The duplicate should be set to Hard Mix. Then lower the Fill value until you get a pleasing blend. Try going all the way to zero and fading the values back up rather than trying to find the right balance starting from 100. Doing so will ensure that you don't overdo the effect.

When you have a nice balance of contrast, lower the Opacity value to reduce some of the saturation. For additional refinement, drag the Blend If sliders.

An alternative approach is to use this method for balancing low-contrast image areas by applying a layer mask and painting in the effect. To do this, fill the layer mask with black, and then use a soft-edged brush to paint white directly on the mask to selectively reveal the adjustments. ■

You have several ways to customize a pseudo-halftone effect in Photoshop. Although you can apply the Color Halftone filter directly, I prefer having more control when executing the effect. The following technique uses random noise and allows for easy variations. It doesn't produce a true halftone simulation, but it's still a great look for portraits with large dynamic range, and is also useful for creating minimalist looks in high-key images.

This effect looks best on high-resolution images, typically print sizes of at least four or five inches on a side at 300 dpi. Smaller images, or those intended for screen output, should be scaled up or use much smaller values for noise and opacity settings. Scale your image with caution because doing so introduces artifacts; but the effect here should give you a lot of latitude to hide any imperfections caused by making the image larger.

Create a new layer above your background image and fill it with 50% gray. Name this layer *Noise*.

Change Noise's blend mode to Hard Mix to reduce your image to six colors plus black and white.

Choose Filter > Noise > Add Noise to apply some noise to the Noise layer. In the dialog box, choose between 50% and 100% values, with Gaussian and Monochromatic selected.

Finally, apply a small blur to Halftone using Filter > Blur > Gaussian Blur. ■

1 Create a blank layer above your image, and fill with 50% gray.

2 Change the gray layer's blend mode to Hard Mix.

3 Add noise to the gray layer (50% to 100%).

4 Apply Gaussian blur to the noise layer (2 px to 10 px).

5 Reduce Fill Opacity to about 70% or less.

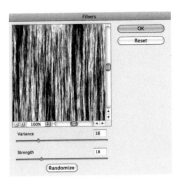

The Hard Mix Noise technique showed you how to build a color "halftone" noise effect. The following variations don't take much work, but they give you lots of flexibility in realizing a wide range of looks.

Follow the steps for Hard Mix Noise, but try these alternative techniques individually or in combination:

- Lower the Fill slider value (not Opacity) to allow Hard Mix to blend some of the base colors. This variation is especially good for black-and-white images as it generates some wonderful transitions and grain.

- Insert a Black & White adjustment layer between the background and noise layers.

- Replace the Add Noise step with Render > Fibers, and then choose Edit > Fade Effect and set Mode to Soft Light with a lower Opacity value. Finish by lowering the Fill percentage.

While the example image uses all three of these in combination, each of these variations is useful when used individually.

Virtually any pattern also can be used on the Noise layer as long as some variation is present in the gray levels; but typically, softer edges and lower contrast patterns work best. The presence of color will, of course, result in another effect altogether, so experiment by adding a Hue/Saturation adjustment layer clipped to Noise, and choose Colorize. ∎

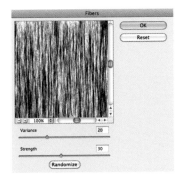

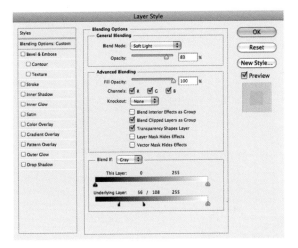

You can synthesize a gentle rain quickly using this simple technique.

Above your image, add a new layer filled with 50% gray. Make sure your foreground and background colors are the default black and white. (Press D to reset them.)

Choose Filter > Render > Fibers to apply the Fibers filter to the gray layer. You are creating a harsh transition with many thin lines, or filaments. Start with a Variance of about 20 and a Strength of 30. Click the Randomize button until you get a fairly balanced look, and click OK.

Double-click the layer to open the Advanced Blending dialog box. Under Blend If, drag the This Layer black sliders until you have the amount of rain you want. Hold down Alt (Windows) or Option (Mac OS), and drag one side of the sliders to soften the transition.

Here's the sneaky part: Create a new, blank layer above the rain layer. Shift-click the rain layer to select it with the blank layer. Press Control+E or Command+E to merge the layers.

This technique traps the transparency created by the Blend If sliders. Change the Blend Mode of the merged layer to Soft Light. For variation, you can apply a small Gaussian blur followed by a slight vertical Motion blur, and lower the opacity of the rain layer. ■

1   Fill a blank layer with 50% gray.

2   With foreground and background set to Black and White, apply a Fibers filter. Use 20 for Variance and about 30 for Strength.

3   Apply Blend If to This Layer to turn black transparent on the Fibers-filtered layer.

4   Create a blank layer above the Fibers-filtered layer and merge the two.

5   Change the Blend Mode to Soft Light.

6   Apply Gaussian and Motion blur to taste, lower Opacity.

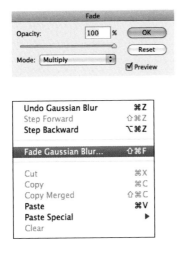

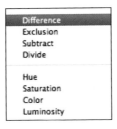

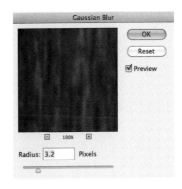

An alternative to the preceding rain recipe generates a soft rain pattern against a black background. This is useful for compositing against darker images, or as a background on a stormy night.

Start with a 50% gray layer, and apply the Fibers filter as in Gentle Rain 1. Then, choose Edit > Fade Fibers and set Mode to Multiply and Opacity to 100% to darken the effect a bit. Click OK.

Next, apply a small Gaussian blur of about two to four pixels. Again, choose the Edit > Fade Fibers command, but this time set Mode to Difference and Opacity to 100%.

You now have a great rain texture against a dark background. You can now place this over a photo and set the blend mode of the rain to Screen. ∎

1 Create a blank layer, fill with 50% gray

2 With foreground and background set to Black and White, apply a Fibers filter. Use 20 for Variance and about 30 for Strength.

3 Use Edit > Fade Fibers and set to Multiply and 100% Opacity.

4 Blur a small amount with Filter > Blur > Gaussian Blur.

5 Edit > Fade Gaussian Blur set to Difference and 100% Opacity.

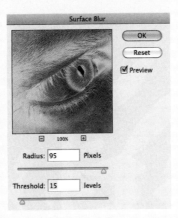

You've got a sharp image, but you want it to be razor-sharp. Freaky Details uses a little-known trick with blend modes: You can assign a blend mode to a layer group. The change in blend mode sums the blending in the group and applies the blend input to the group.

First, create two copies of your image and combine them into a single group. Set the group's blend mode to Overlay, and leave the bottom copy blend mode set to Normal.

The top layer must be a Smart Object, so choose Filters > Convert for Smart Filters. Open the new Smart Object, and then invert it. Save and close the object to return to your original document.

Change the Smart Object's blend mode to Vivid Light, and apply a Smart Blur filter by choosing Filter > Blur > Smart Blur. Use a fairly high pixel value (95 was used for this image), and start the Threshold around 15. You want a smooth surface with hard edges. Perform this step last to see and adjust the effect in real time. The advantage to using Smart Objects is that you can change the values whenever you like.

CALVIN HOLLYWOOD
CALVINHOLLYWOOD.DE

1   Duplicate the background layer twice.
2   Select the top two layers and press Ctrl+G or Command+G to group them.
3   Set the group blend mode to Overlay.
4   Convert the top layer to a Smart Object. Open it, and then invert it.
5   Save the Smart Object, and close it.
6   In the original document, apply a Surface Blur filter to the Smart Object.
7   Change the Smart Object's blend mode to Vivid Light.

CHAPTER 5
DESIGN, PAINTING, & ILLUSTRATION

Much of the Photoshop world is dominated by artists who never apply the software to photographs. Painters, designers, and illustrators—this section is for you.

While I'm relatively new to 3D in Photoshop, it is very intriguing when applied to my method and adds a new dimension to my work. Every piece I create is an experiment in pushing visual as well as technical boundaries, often using blend modes to help capture the depth of color and shadows.

I add layers upon layers in building these images and stop only when I feel that the message relays the vision. Some of these blends are six layers deep, each layer having a different blend mode.

Each layer and/or blend mode is dependent upon the other. Therefore, many of the layers appear out of sequence; but due to the layer on top or underneath, the image blending works visually. All settings are visual and not calculated.

My ideas start with one simple object and build from that. Although each effort doesn't always work to satisfaction, the experimentation adds to the horizon of visions upon which other images grow. "Playful but message related" is where all my images start and conclude.

HOW IT WAS DONE

Here is the combination of layers and blend modes I used for this image:

- SS first five layers
  - Ground planes—two layers
    - Bottom is Normal at 49%
    - Top is Normal at 100%
  - Top flowers—two layers
    - Bottom is darker color at 20%
    - Top is Linear Light at 88%
  - Bottom flower/foliage layer
    - Luminosity at 76%
- SS bug layers
  - Bottom is Linear Burn at 100%
  - Top is Soft Light at 100%
- SS floating flower layers
  - Perspective grid layer (AI vector image)
    - Luminosity at 20%
  - 3D render of flower
    - Normal at 100%
  - Flower shadow—three layers
    - Bottom is Color at 100%
    - Middle is Subtract at 32%
    - Top is Hue at 76%
- SS 3D ball layers
  - Bottom layer is Normal at 100%
  - Middle is Soft Light at 100%
  - Top is Hard Light at 30%
  - Lower-left 3D flowers and grid layers
    - Two flowers set to Normal at 100%
    - Flower is Grid Luminosity at 100%
    - Single flower at bottom is Luminosity at 100%

By blending layers, I am able to marry images one to another. In lots of cases, I create duplicates of certain layers and change the blend modes in each to realize the look and feel that I envision, sometimes two to eight layers deep. Layers are not merged as this can change the effect, so a drawing file consists of many layers to achieve the desired visual impact. This process is pursued by intuition and not by design or strategy.

KAT GILBERT
INTHEWOODONLINE.COM

Blend modes applied to the Brush tool via the options bar offer unique opportunities for painting on a single layer. This trick takes the technique a bit further and shows how to set up a custom brush to take more advantage of Photoshop's painting capabilities.

We'll create a custom brush, first. Start by creating a new shape on a blank layer. For this example, I used a preset butterfly shape (found in the Nature set that installs with Photoshop) in a square document of 4 inches by 4 inches. However, you could also use a square or elliptical marquee. With the selection active, create another blank layer and begin painting with black using a large, soft brush set to Dissolve mode in the options bar. Just paint lightly along the edges of the selection as if you were tracing it loosely, leaving a lot of open areas.

For this example, I duplicated the painted layer, added a small amount of blur, then merged the blurred and unblurred layers. Keep the selection active (or reselect, if necessary, by Command-clicking or Ctrl-clicking the layer thumbnail) after you are finished painting, choose Edit > Define Brush Preset, and name your new brush.

Open the Brush Presets panel and scroll to the bottom of the list to find your new brush. The new brush will be selected by default after creating it. Open the Brush panel to refine your

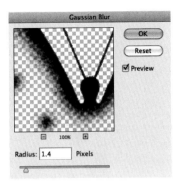

brush settings. I like to adjust Shape Dynamics, Dual Brush, and Color Dynamics, and increase spacing on the Brush Tip Shape tab to behave as if I'm scattering individual marks as I paint.

Under Brush Dynamics, choose another brush shape, and set the Dual Brush blend mode option to Linear Height. For this image, I chose the 59 px Spatter brush marker. For Color Dynamics, set everything to 0 except Foreground/Background Jitter, which should be about 50%, and Purity, which should be 100%.

In your document, turn off all layers except the background layer and create a new blank layer. Choose two complementary colors as foreground and background color, and start painting. In the current example, the foreground is yellow and the background is cyan. The result is a bunch of marks in various shades of yellow and green.

To use more of the background color, set the Hue Jitter to 100%, or press X to swap the foreground and background colors. You can, and should, change the Brush blend mode option while playing with this technique. Start with Color to allow overlapping marks to blend.

As a bonus, you can use the Clear and Behind blend mode options. If you lay down so many marks that they start filling in or getting too busy, switch to Clear mode, and erase some of the paint using the same marker shape. ■

Once I have the majority of a painting done, I go back for a refinement pass to paint in color highlights. This is done on blank layers set to a variety of blend modes, including stacks of layers with different modes. Here are some details on how I work.

For the face in this tree, I needed some extra color to help set the evening mood. On a blank layer set to Color blend mode, I began to paint with a soft brush using a medium blue. This pass was rough, just to get the general shape of the color areas. It was important not to fill in the entire area at once.

When I had the major areas filled in, I applied a blur to the layer to soften the transitions and let some of the base color blend with the highlights. From there, the Eraser (E) or Smudge tools took care of smaller details.

In general, when I need to apply a stronger effect that includes more of the base colors, I use Overlay blend mode on the layer. However, at times I really need some drama, as with these fairy wings. I gave these a pervasive glow using a layer stack of different modes with slightly different colors on each.

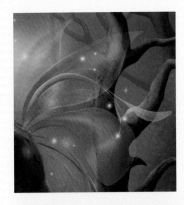 

The modes used for these images were Vivid Light, Soft Light, and Color Dodge. Painting directly on layers set to various blend modes gives more control and a broader range of looks than painting directly on the image.

JOHN SHANNON
JESHANNON.COM

No Map

Fibers Only

Normal @ 50 %

Multiply

Screen

Overlay

Difference

Divide

3D models use a variety of skins to cover meshes, or pieces, of the overall model. These skins are called *textures*, and a set of textures is generally referred to as a *material*. A full explanation of 3D tools and materials is beyond the scope of this book; but for those who understand the basics of 3D modeling in Photoshop, I did want to point out a few tricks for generating and editing 3D materials, specifically *depth maps*.

If you need to get up to speed on 3D, see the reference section in the appendix for some great online resources. (Note that 3D functionality is available only in the Extended versions of Photoshop.)

Depth maps use levels of gray to indicate height, or displacement from a center point. Black represents the lowest point, and white represents the highest. Although Photoshop allows you to work in Grayscale mode, we want to take full advantage of blending modes so we'll use RGB as our color space.

To set up this file, I created a new document and filled a blank layer with 50% gray, and then created a cylinder mesh as a depth map (3D > New Mesh From Layer > Depth Map To > Cylinder). The gray layer set the diameter of the cylinder to the middle allowable value. When the depth map was opened, this gray layer was the base.

In the depth map file, I added a new layer, filled it with gray, and then rendered Fibers with black and white as the background and foreground colors. I lowered opacity of the Fibers layer to about 17%. This will be my foundation texture for this example. Above the Fibers layer, I filled another layer with gray and rendered some basic clouds.

Look at the effects on the depth map when the Clouds layer is given various blend modes and opacities or fills. Each sample shows the cylinder with the depth map applied, and the depth map itself is in the background. ■

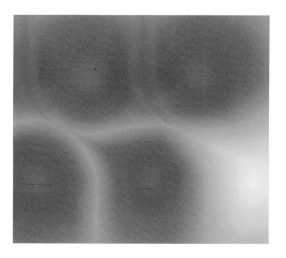
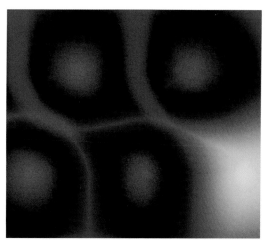

Sometimes I rely on randomness to get past a creative block. This little trick is one way to do this and also realize some very nice graphic results. The technique is simple, and can be controlled as much or as little as you desire.

Starting with a blank canvas (or a blank layer above a filled background), choose the Gradient tool (G) and set its blend mode to Difference in the options bar. For this example, I used the Radial Gradient tool with yellow in the center (foreground) and cyan at the edges (background). To create a pattern, set up guides and drag out gradients at regular intervals. If you find that the color hides your guides, turn on Snapping in the View menu. Also, be sure to overlap your gradients a bit so the color variations interact.

This technique can be repeated and varied in any number of ways. Choose the starting colors carefully and keep the History panel open. Each time you drag out a gradient with Difference mode, the colors will reverse, so you may have to drag another gradient or use an adjustment layer to change colors. Try starting with 80% and 20% gray, and then add a Color or Gradient adjustment layer.

For further experimentation, duplicate the layer and tinker with the blend modes, invert it, use Advanced Blending, and so on. The example images show the results duplicated, inverted, and then set to Subtract. Think of this as finger painting with Photoshop. ∎

A client once asked me to create an animated promotional video with a stylized cartoon look and feel. Since I was using Adobe Flash Professional for the character design and animation, I decided to keep things simple and remain in Flash for the background design. But I also wanted to apply some texture to separate the animated character from its environment; and to remove the flat, hard-edged quality of the vector-drawn background. Adding texture can also contribute a little depth and interest.

First, I exported the background from Flash to PNG format.

In Photoshop, I opened the PNG image along with two different textures, each on its own layer.

I duplicated the background layer, chose Filter > Artistic > Smudge Stick, and set the layer opacity of the duplicate to 50%. The blend mode was set to Overlay to more effectively blend the duplicate with the original background.

Combining the Smudge Stick filter with the Overlay blend mode and transparency created a subtle texture, as if the image was drawn on rough paper. But for this project, the effect was a little too subtle.

Next, I wanted to blend my two paper textures into the background, so the first texture layer was set to Divide blend mode with an opacity of 32%.

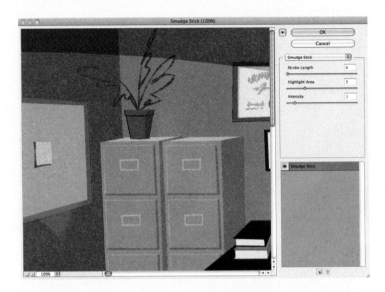

To blend the second texture, I might have used a single texture, but I prefer to layer several textures with varying degrees of opacity to build up complicated effects in subtle ways. I set the blend mode of the second texture to Color Burn to produce a very dark and muddy effect. Lowering the opacity to about 20% resulted in a very rich background with some subtle texture throughout. The colors of the final background were rich, yet no detail was lost.

Using blend modes, I can now design vector-based backgrounds that look and feel as if they were created using a raster-based program or even hand painted. The best part is, I can return to the original vector artwork and scale it to any size. Any new size I create I can open in Photoshop and place on a layer below any two texture files that already have blend modes and opacity applied.

CHRIS GEORGENES
MUDBUBBLE.COM

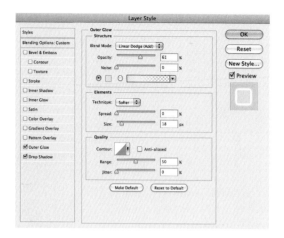

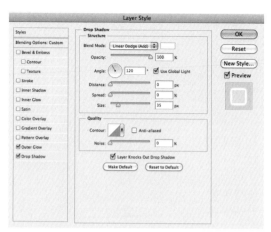

Blend modes are also found in Photoshop's layer styles. This technique is one of many that produces a glowing dust effect, which works best against darker backgrounds. The file is layered up, too, so you have a lot of flexibility. The example image is about 2000 x 3000 pixels, so the pixel scales will have to be adjusted for your specific image dimensions.

With a blank layer created above your background image, use a small scatter brush to paint a trail of white dots. In this example, I used a brush size of about 8 px, set to 135% scatter. Because I use a digital tablet with pressure sensitivity, I have turned on brush dynamics to vary the marker size and opacity.

Once you have the trail in place, or at least a sample so you can see the effect, it's time to create the layer style. Double-click the layer thumbnail to open the Advanced Blending dialog box, and set up the following layer effects:

- Outer Glow

- Drop Shadow

For Outer Glow, choose a bright, saturated color. For this image, I used a bright yellow (255, 252, 0). Set the blend mode to Linear Dodge (Add), and lower the opacity to 50 to 60%. Finally, set the Spread to 0 and the Size to 18 px.

Open up the Drop Shadow effect, and also set its blend mode to Linear Dodge. Opacity should be 100%. Choose White as the effect color. Distance and Spread should be 0, while Size was 35 px for this example image.

Setting the Distance to 0 effectively makes Drop Shadow a second glow, so you have more flexibility in combining colors. Contour can also be adjusted if you want a more obvious transition and glow area.

To finish this picture, I also added a layer set to Overlay blend mode. Using the Dodge and Burn technique, I painted with dark gray and white with a brush set to 10% opacity to build up glow on the objects around the trail, and to drop a little faery dust on the trail itself. This helps sell the idea of the trail interacting with the environment. Because the blend mode is Overlay, the glow will have a stronger effect on lighter areas, so darks are left alone, increasing the feeling of depth.

This same effect can be applied to solid lines. Add an Inner Glow style to give a 3D, tube-like look using a slightly contrasting color for shading. If you draw the line with 50% gray, include a Color Overlay style to refine the color to suit your image. ■

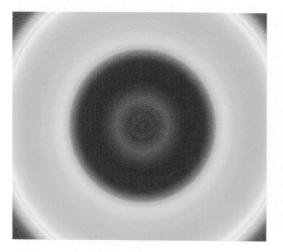

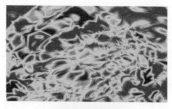

One of my favorite blend mode tricks (albeit a bit frivolous) is to use the paintbrush set with Difference. This technique allows you to create random patterns and textures that can be useful for a variety of effects, especially when you're working in 3D.

The basic effect is created by starting with a gradient. A radial, full-spectrum gradient is perfect. Paint over it with several colors using the Brush tool (B) set to Difference. You'll see the colors start to smear and blend as you apply more brush strokes.

You might look at the final result and ask, "How is that useful?" When you're looking for quick ways to apply random colors, the answer is that it can be very useful. For example, let's constrain the colors a bit so that we end up with something like the brightly colored red and yellow image.

We could use the Linear Light blend mode to blend it with a clouds layer and turn the shades of gray into flames. In this example, I seemingly set an old map of Chicago on fire!

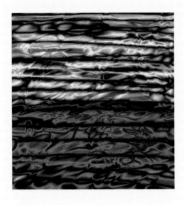

When you're working in 3D, this technique allows you to produce random, organic-looking texture maps to apply to 3D objects. For example, if you're using Digital Anarchy's 3D Invigorator you could apply this wavelike grayscale texture as a bump map or reflectivity map. In the first 3D image, I used the texture as both bump and reflection maps. In the second 3D image, it's used to create a very convincing reflection by itself.

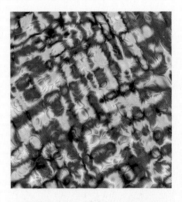

This technique takes a little bit of practice to understand how different colors will affect the texture. If you just want random colors, grab a color, paint some strokes with it, grab another color, paint with it, and repeat until the canvas is completely covered. If you want controlled colors, just use a Gradient Map adjustment layer to change the colors, as in converting a multi-color image to use blues.

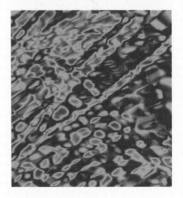

JIM TIERNEY
DIGITALANARCHY.COM

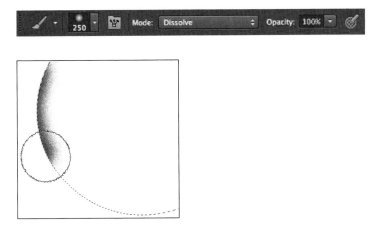

I used to love watching airbrush artists set up frisket or masking material and create soft edges not by blending, but by allowing only a little bit of overspray into solid areas. In Photoshop, you can create a similar but still unique look using the Dissolve blend mode and a soft brush.

The idea is to paint with active selections turned on, which act as a live and temporary mask. To start, choose the Brush tool (B), and make it large and very soft on the edges. Start painting on a new layer to get a feel for where the scattered dots show up. Dissolve works with transparency, so the softer the edge of the brush, the more variation you will get in the distribution of random pixels.

Now use the Marquee tool (M) to drag out a rectangular or elliptical selection. With the selection still active, return to the Brush tool and start painting around the *outside* of your selection so that just a tiny bit of the brush intrudes, leaving specks of paint. You will get a wonderful masked edge filled with the paint you chose. For the sample image, I also used the Pen tool to create paths, and then converted them to selections.

You should know a couple of things about this technique. First, when using Dissolve mode on the brush, you are free to change the blend mode and opacity of the layer independently. You can also blur the results if you choose.

Second, because the Dissolve mode leaves transparent areas, you can also switch to Behind blend mode for the brush and fill in some areas with different color without altering the pixels already laid down. That also means you can stack up layers and build up a scene very quickly.

Finally, the size of the speckles left by Dissolve is related to the size of your document. The example image was sized about 7 inches by 9 inches at 300 dpi. Typical web graphics have much lower resolution and smaller size so the pixels will appear much larger. If you are going to produce images for screen display, consider working at a larger size, and then saving a flattened version before scaling down the image. This will give you a much finer dot size. ■

The most useful Photoshop blend mode for me is Hard Light. It makes midtones invisible, while retaining highlights and shadows. So, you can paint a mid (50%) gray area to use as a selection area, and then add whichever textures you want on top: Clouds, Noise, whatever. When you change the layer mode to Hard Light, all the gray disappears leaving just the texture.

In this example image, I created an oil spill by painting an area in 50% gray, and then added a little shading using the Dodge and Burn tools. The Plastic Wrap filter does a good job of adding gloss, which makes the whole effect look shiny. Note that Plastic Wrap is a tricky filter to manipulate. You might find that you have to run it, undo, adjust the shading, and then run the filter again several times before you get the result you want.

Changing the layer mode to Hard Light hides the gray, leaving just the shine. Here, I used Color Balance to add a red and yellow tint to the gray, and I also distorted a copy of the background to create a refractive effect.

STEVE CAPLIN
HOWTOCHEATINPHOTOSHOP.COM

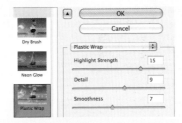

1. On a blank layer above the background, paint an area with 50% gray.
2. Set the blend mode of the fill layer to Hard Light. Use the Dodge and Burn tools to create some highlight and shadow areas.
3. Apply Filter > Artistic > Plastic Wrap. (It's now in the Filter Gallery.)
4. Add a Color Balance adjustment layer.

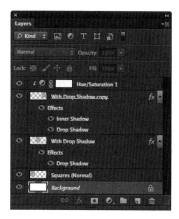

Generating repeating patterns in Photoshop can be tedious work, even with something as simple as checkerboard squares. The next several recipes show you how to quickly develop repeating patterns and textures.

Start with a square document with a white background. Select 50% gray as your foreground color by clicking the foreground swatch and entering *H:0, S:0, B:50* in the dialog box. Click OK.

Select the Gradient tool (G), and click the gradient sample in the options bar to open the dialog box. Choose the Transparent Stripes preset, and close the dialog box. Make sure the Transparency box in the options bar is selected.

On the blank layer, hold down Shift and drag from the left edge to the right. You can use guides and enable snapping to get more precise results. In the Gradient tool options bar, choose Divide from the blend modes pop-up.

Drag from top to bottom on your canvas. You now have an evenly spaced checkerboard pattern. Clip a Hue/Saturation adjustment layer, and click the Colorize box to control the color.

Note that not all the white squares are transparent. Apply a drop shadow to the gradient layer to see this. If you want to remove the transparency, merge the gradient and background layers. Be sure to remove any layer effects if you don't want them baked into your image. ■

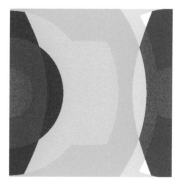

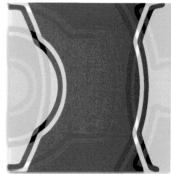

You can create cool retro outlines with a little imagination and blur. Start with a square document, and add a blank layer on top. Choose the Gradient tool, and from the options bar, select the Spectrum gradient from the defaults. Finally, choose the Radial setting. Be sure the Gradient tool's blend mode is set to Normal.

Use horizontal and vertical guides along the edges and center for reference.

Using the Gradient tool, hold down Shift (to keep the movement perfectly horizontal) and drag from the center left to the center right edge. From the tool options bar, choose Hard Mix from the pop-up blend modes menu. On the same layer, drag a new gradient from center right to center left.

Duplicate the gradient layer and invert the colors by pressing Ctrl+I (Windows) or Command+I (Mac). Set this duplicate's blend mode to Vivid Light. Give the layer a small Gaussian blur—just enough to remove the hard edges—and then apply a tiny bit more. Voila! You should now have thick outlines around the major shapes. But they're still jagged, so let's fix that.

Select both gradient layers and merge them. (Press Ctrl+E/ Command+E.) Now give the merged layer about half the blur you applied last time. Duplicate this layer again, and set the top layer's blend mode to Vivid Light. Smoove! ■

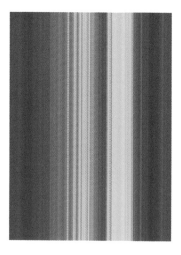
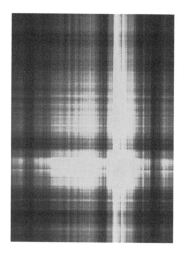

Fabric and crosshatch textures are amazingly easy to generate using some tricks with gradients. The basic idea is to blend noise gradients with each other, rotated at 90 degrees.

Load a noise gradient by choosing the Gradient tool and clicking the arrow next to the gradient sample. This opens the Presets panel. In the upper right of the panel, click the small gear to open another menu. Choose Noise Samples, and then choose Append to add this sample to your current preset list.

The image shown here uses the Fade command. To the left is a basic noise gradient dragged out from left to right. The middle image was made by then dragging the same gradient on the same layer from top to bottom, and immediately choosing Edit > Fade Gradient > Overlay.

The image on the right used the same method, but with Lighten as the blend mode.

Creating the rotated gradient on another layer (copy to a new layer, and choose Edit > Transform > Rotate 90 CW) preserves flexibility; or to speed up the process when you know what you want, you can select the blend mode directly from the Gradient options bar.

There are an amazing number of variations on this technique, including applying a Gradient Map adjustment layer, converting to grayscale for use as 3D textures, and scrolling through various blend modes. ∎

 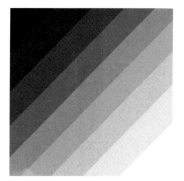 

To perform a variation on the Squares pattern technique, posterize a linear gradient. Starting with a 4-inch by 4-inch square document, choose the Gradient tool (G), and drag a linear two-color gradient from the upper-left corner down to the lower right. For flexibility in coloring, use 80% gray for the foreground and 20% gray for the background.

Create bands from this gradient using a Posterize adjustment layer. Select six to ten levels, and click OK. Merge the layer with its adjustment layer by clicking one and Shift-clicking the other, then press Ctrl+E (Windows) or Command+E (Mac). Optionally, you can convert the layer to a Smart Object and apply the Poster Edges filter under the Artistic filter group.

Duplicate the layer by pressing Ctrl/Command+J, and rotate it 90 degrees clockwise by choosing Edit > Transform > Rotate > Rotate 90 CW. Finally, set the duplicate's blend mode to Difference.

You now have a pattern of squares in several levels of gray. The basic technique also can be extended to other gradients, but works best with solid two-color gradients. Try a Radial gradient, and instead of rotating, move the duplicate halfway to one side of the canvas. Or use the Transparent Stripes gradient instead of a duplicate of the base layer.

Merging the layers captures the pattern, which you can then duplicate and use again. Add color and other adjustment layers, change blend modes and opacity, or just keep building. ∎

Flat Color   Soft Light   Final

As a cartoonist and illustrator, I'm always working on deadline. To that end, I've spent years developing efficient methods of drawing and painting in Photoshop. One blend mode I consistently rely on to create versatile light and shadow is Soft Light.

What I like most about Soft Light is that it basically does the same thing as the Dodge and Burn tools, but with a lot more finesse. Once I have a cartoon or illustration with the flat color filled in, I'll Ctrl-click (Windows) or Command-click (Mac) the layer thumbnail to select everything within the layer. After creating a new layer set to Soft Light blend mode, I can paint with black and white to add light and shadow to the flat color layer beneath while leaving the original layer untouched.

Using different brushes set to different opacities, the added light and shadow can be quite obvious or very subtle. I can also adjust the opacity of the layer itself to vary the amount of the effect. Once I get the darks and lights looking right, I combine the layers by merging them (press Ctrl/Command+E with the highlight layers selected), and then paint by continually sampling the new colors created while painting with the Soft Light layer blend mode.

PATRICK LAMONTAGNE
CARTOONINK.COM

PART III
BLEND MODES IN DEPTH

Understanding the mechanics of blend modes can take some time. This section discusses how blend modes work "behind the scenes." A great way to fully understand these mechanics is to open a reference file and look for the described effects as you explore the following chapters.

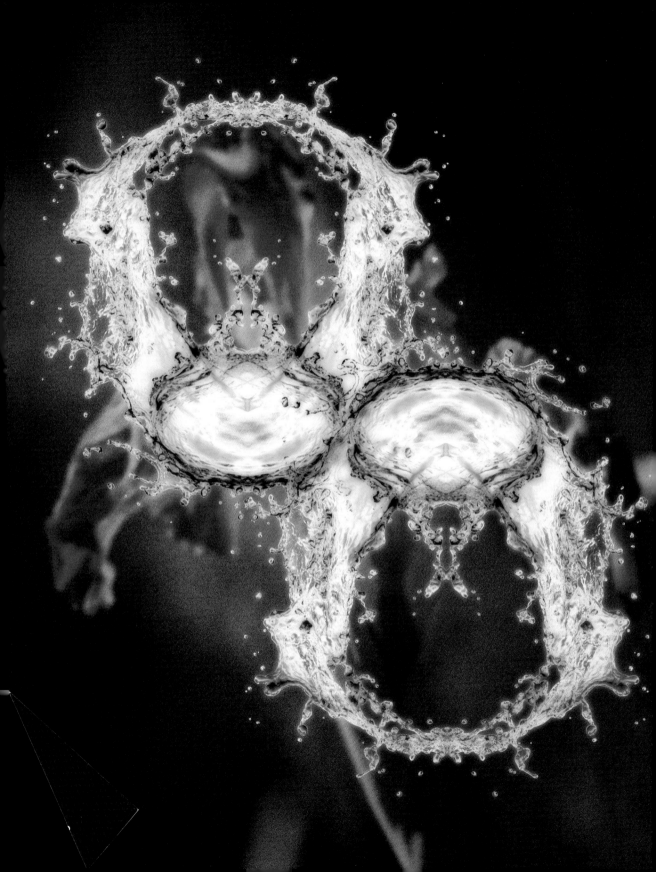

CHAPTER 6
DECODING BLEND MODES

Before you begin exploring the blend modes listing in Chapter 7, you'll need to understand some of the conventions, procedures, and thinking that went into its creation. Along the way you'll also learn a bit about the math behind the magic of blend modes.

UNDERSTANDING THE LISTINGS

This listing of blend modes in Chapter 7 includes the Adobe Help file entry, my own thoughts and descriptions, and an equation based on observation of blend mode effects. Adobe's actual blend mode equations are proprietary, so the equations were tested by sampling the result of a blend between known colors and opacities. This is not always an accurate method, but does yield a reasonable starting point for examining how blend modes are calculated. The equations presented are meant only as a reference for those who are interested in the mathematics of blend modes. (See the sidebar, "Blend Mode Math," for further information.)

Each entry is presented like this:

Darken, Commutative, 50% Gray, Fill

The first item is the general group. In the blend modes pop-up menu on the Layers panel, separator lines combine the modes into groups. The first two modes, Normal and Dissolve, are in the Normal group. The remaining groups are Darken, Lighten, Contrast, Comparison, and Compositing. These group names should be self-explanatory as to the modes they contain; but if you are unclear, a quick look at the entries will help clarify their functions.

Commutative indicates that the layer order does not matter for a given pair of layers. You will get the same result regardless which of the layers is on top so long as the top one gets the blend mode change. *Non-commutative* label indicates that layer order does influence the result.

The next item is the neutral color, that is, the color that has no effect on the output. Typically, this will be black, white, or 50% gray. Some modes have no neutral color. You can determine a mode's neutral color by Alt-clicking (Windows) or Option-clicking (Mac) the New Layer icon in the bottom of the Layers panel. A dialog box appears with the option to set the layer's blend mode and offers to fill the layer with that blend mode's neutral color.

A handful of modes behave differently when you adjust Opacity and Fill values. That is, adjusting opacity for these blend modes gives a different result than adjusting fill. This is a handy thing to know because it gives you additional control over refining your blends. The modes that do this are labeled as *Fill*.

BLEND MODE MATH

Blend modes are executed using math, of course, but showing the mathematical details of each mode doesn't really help most folks understand their function. And the users who are interested in seeing the math at work will probably need much more accurate equations than I can provide here. For example, several Internet sites show procedural approaches to blend modes that include code and programming languages, and they are likely to be more helpful for users who are programming plug-ins or doing technical analysis.

However, I don't feel a discussion on blend modes is complete without a little peek at the numbers. Let's consider the Multiply blend mode, for example. The basic idea is that the gray value in a channel of one layer is literally multiplied by the gray value in another layer's analagous channel. That is, the gray value of a pixel in the red channel of the top layer is compared with the same pixel value in the red channel in the bottom layer.

Each channel is considered individually and multiplied by taking the percent value of the gray level for each channel. Ready to get your geek on? For an 8-bit image, if a given pixel on one layer is 182, and the other layer is 94:

$182 / 256 = 71\%$

$94 / 256 = 37\%$

$0.71 * 0.37 = 0.26$

$0.26 * 256 = 67$

So, the resulting gray value for that channel is 67, which is fairly dark considering the two inputs. Some blend modes use composite information: the data from each channel in a layer is summed and used for blending, which gives a different result than using individual channels.

REFERENCE IMAGES

Every description includes a set of reference images made up of two layers whose only difference is that the blend mode of the top layer changes to match the entry. All of the sample images were created in 16-bit RGB color space, but it's important to note that there are differences in gamut between RGB, CMYK, and Photoshop's native LAB space. Bit depth also affects which blend modes are available, but they behave in a similar way when applicable (see "32-, 16-, and 8-bit Images" for more information).

NOTE For more information on LAB, see Dan Margulis' excellent book titled, *Photoshop LAB Color: The Canyon Conundrum and Other Adventures in the Most Powerful Colorspace* (Peachpit Press). Dan covers pretty much everything you need to know about LAB. For the purposes of this book, just know that when you need to work with blend modes you need to switch to RGB.

32-, 16-, AND 8-BIT IMAGES

32-bit images are intended for High Dynamic Range (HDR) processing. Due to the nature of 32-bit processing, negative values can be present in the channels. In fact, the expanded dynamic range implies an infinite range going both positive *and* negative. Many of the blend modes available in Photoshop are not configured for this range of numbers.

Why use higher bit depths? Put succinctly, the bit depth determines the range of possible colors available to your image. 8-bit depth is standard, offering 16.8 million colors, while 16-bit gives over 281 trillion colors. The human eye can not see all of these colors, even in 8-bit space, but calculations in Photoshop can certainly take advantage of the added detail.

The additional bit depth gives you finer control in refining your colors, tones, and brightness.

When using blend modes, you should start at the highest bit depth you need in RGB and complete as much work as you can in that color space. When you need to use more blend modes, save a copy of your work and lower the bit depth. (Most modes work in 16-bit, except as noted.) Finally, if you need to convert to another color space, flatten your image first.

I have included URLs in the appendix that discuss bit depth in ways that are outside the scope of this book. Some blend modes use different equations for each bit depth to produce similar results.

NOTE The center point of 128 for 8-bit images is considered 50% gray, or neutral. The real situation is a bit more complex, but we'll leave the details to computer scientists. What you need to know is that the closer you get to 128, the less drastic the change when you invert a given color. But don't forget that each channel, RGB, has its own range of 0 to 255.

NOTE On my website (lightningsymphony.com), you can download these images as PSD files.

The two base triangle images are identical to each other, representing a step-wise spectrum of RGB colors. Above the triangle labeled Self is an exact copy of the base, just in a new layer. The one labeled Inverted is a copy that has been inverted in Photoshop by color using the Ctrl/Cmd+I keyboard shortcut. This command inverts the Red, Green, and Blue values (for RGB images) around the 8-bit image center point of 128. When you fill a layer with Red (R=255, G=0, B=0), and then invert it, you get Cyan (R=0, G=255, B=255).

It's important to note that while inverting Red gives us Cyan, these triangles are still in RGB color space. Cyan in RGB looks quite different from Cyan in CMYK. These example images in Chapter 7 were built in RGB (Adobe RGB, specifically), but were converted to CMYK for the printing process.

At the bottom of each page is a pair of squares. Both have the same pattern:

Red – Yellow – Green – Cyan – Blue – Magenta

COLOR INVERSION

When I talk about inverting colors here, I am not talking about fractions. Think of the range from 1 to 256 as a number line, with 128 in the middle. (The actual values are 0 to 255, thereby are 256 *units*.) When you choose any other number along the line, it is located some distance from 128. Going the same distance from 128 in the opposite direction locates the inverted color.

For example, let's choose a value of 74, which is 54 units away from 128 (128–74 = 54). Now we add that result to 128 to get the inverse color: 128+54 = 182. This is the same as simply subtracting 74 from 256 to get 182.

Another way to think about this is using percentages. Any pixel value you choose from 1 to 256 can be made into a percentage by dividing that value by 256. So, a pixel with a value of 74, regardless of its channel, is 74/256 = 29 percent of that channel's color. Because percent means "part of 100," and because we're dealing with decimals, we can subtract the result from 1: 1–0.29 = 0.71.

Comparing the two methods we get:

128–74 = 54, 128+54 = 182 (or 256–74 = 182)

74/256 = 0.29, 1–0.29 = .71

So, the inverse of 74 is about 182 by the first method, or around 71% of 256 by the second. A quick check shows that 256*0.71 = 182 (rounded to the nearest integer).

This will get you into the ballpark when you are trying to predict an output color. Internally, Photoshop uses the second method with the addition of some sophisticated rounding and truncation methods. The reason for this has to do with both bit depth and color mode mapping, which is outside the scope of this book to discuss. In short, Photoshop needs both a middle value for 50% gray, and can only use whole numbers for bit brightness, so decimals are not allowed.

The examples I present here also use the second method whenever practicable.

The base layer goes from left to right following the preceding pattern. The blend layer is rotated 90 degrees so the same pattern extends from top to bottom.

The more important reason for including the squares here is to show you patterns in the spectra. While not completely practical, these patterns are interesting because it's easy to recognize and remember patterns, and to pick out different behaviors of the various blend modes. And some of the results look really, really cool. The more typical approach of showing two photographs blended together tends to obscure what's really going on with the individual colors. We start by looking at the overall effect on the photos themselves rather than looking at the results of blending two colors.

While writing this book, I considered including more reference images. There are good arguments for including images showing opacity and fill, solid-to-gradient, gray scale, additional color spaces, and so on. In the end, I chose to build and share several reference files on my website. These files will allow you to explore things that are best seen in Photoshop itself, rather than in the static pages of a book in CMYK.

Opacity and fill, for example, are best understood when you are playing with the sliders yourself. This is also true of tools such as Blend If, Fade, and many others. If you are interested in exploring these modes in more detail, you can desconstruct the files I've provided and then build your own set of reference images, specific to your needs and interests.

A quick reference summary of these notes is included in the appendix.

NOTE I had a physics professor who was a big advocate of "twiddling the knobs" during experiments. In Photoshop, doing so is relatively painless and mostly disaster-free, unlike in my physics class. You can freely adjust opacity, fill, and other blending parameters. Grab the files from my website and start twiddling those knobs!

CHAPTER 7
LIST OF BLEND MODES

Every blend mode in Photoshop is listed here for your exploration and review. In addition to providing a handy reference list, we've also allowed room on the pages to make your own notes. Consider keeping track of your favorite techniques for each mode.

ALT/OPTION+SHIFT+N

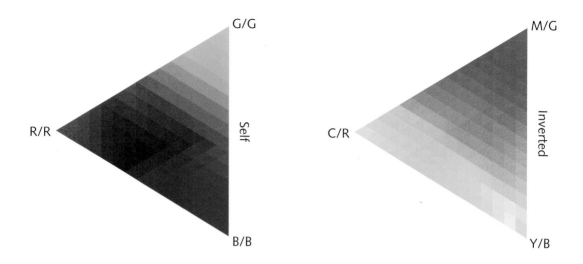

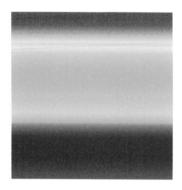

NORMAL, NON-COMMUTATIVE, NONE

Edits or paints each pixel to make it the result color. This is the default mode. (Normal mode is called Threshold when you're working with a bitmapped or indexed-color image.)

Normal blend mode is the basis for all standard editing. It's how you might view a printed picture lying on a table. Applying a mask essentially trims the image, cutting holes in the layer. By adjusting the gray level of a mask, you adjust the mask transparency (the opposite of opacity) with black being 100% transparent, and white being 100% opaque.

Opacity adjustments can also be applied to the layer as a whole, causing anything beneath to show through uniformly. Further, it's possible to combine the effects of a layer mask with layer opacity for more global control over the layer's transparency.

No equation goes with this blend mode, as any blending is simply a function of transparency of one color over another.

NOTE Throughout these listings, keyboard commands for Windows and Mac OS will be abbreviated and combined. Therefore, Alt+Shift+N (Windows) and Option+Shift+N (Mac OS) will be represented by Alt/Option+Shift+N. As noted in General Techniques, you can also scroll forward and backward through the list by activating the Move tool (V), then holding down Shift and pressing + (plus) or – (minus.).

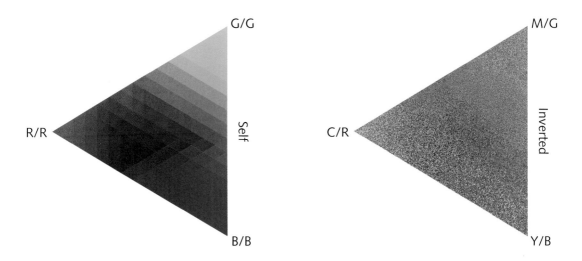

NORMAL, NON-COMMUTATIVE, NONE

Edits or paints each pixel to make it the result color. That result color is a random replacement of the pixels with the base color or the blend color, depending on the opacity at any pixel location.

Use Dissolve when you plan to merge the effect with the base for more complex effects. A great way to use this on an image directly is to duplicate the layer, and apply a solid Fill or Gradient. Then fade the effect using Dissolve, and lower the opacity. Blur again to taste. You can also use this to add noise to a texture base, and then blend the result.

Again, no equation is provided here because the pixels are selected from a random seed that governs which pixels will disappear at a given level of opacity. Dissolve works by generating a 100% random noise pattern. Each pixel gets a value—analagous to a gray level—that is turned off at a specific opacity level. The more that opacity is reduced, the fewer pixels are visible. It is important to be aware that there is no fading of this effect directly.

DARKEN

ALT/OPTION+SHIFT+K

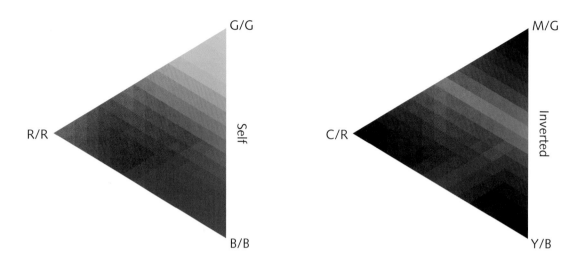

DARKEN, COMMUTATIVE, WHITE

Looks at the color information in each channel, and selects the base or blend color—whichever is darker—as the result color. Pixels lighter than the blend color are replaced, and pixels darker than the blend color do not change.

Output = min(Base, Blend) // Channel operation

While it's not obvious from the help file information, Darken can result in a new color because each channel is compared separately. Consider the following 8-bit example:

Top Layer: R=251, G=175, B=93 (light yellow orange)

Bottom Layer: R=125, G=167, B=217 (pastel cyan)

Result: R=125, G=167, B=93 (light green)

The results can be unexpected! Try using Darken for some compositing work—especially blending textures—because the result of blending may yield a pleasing intermediate color when channels have similar gray values.

This comparison has no effect on a simple self-blend. To see the effect, the two layers must be different in some way.

Darken is not available in L*a*b* space.

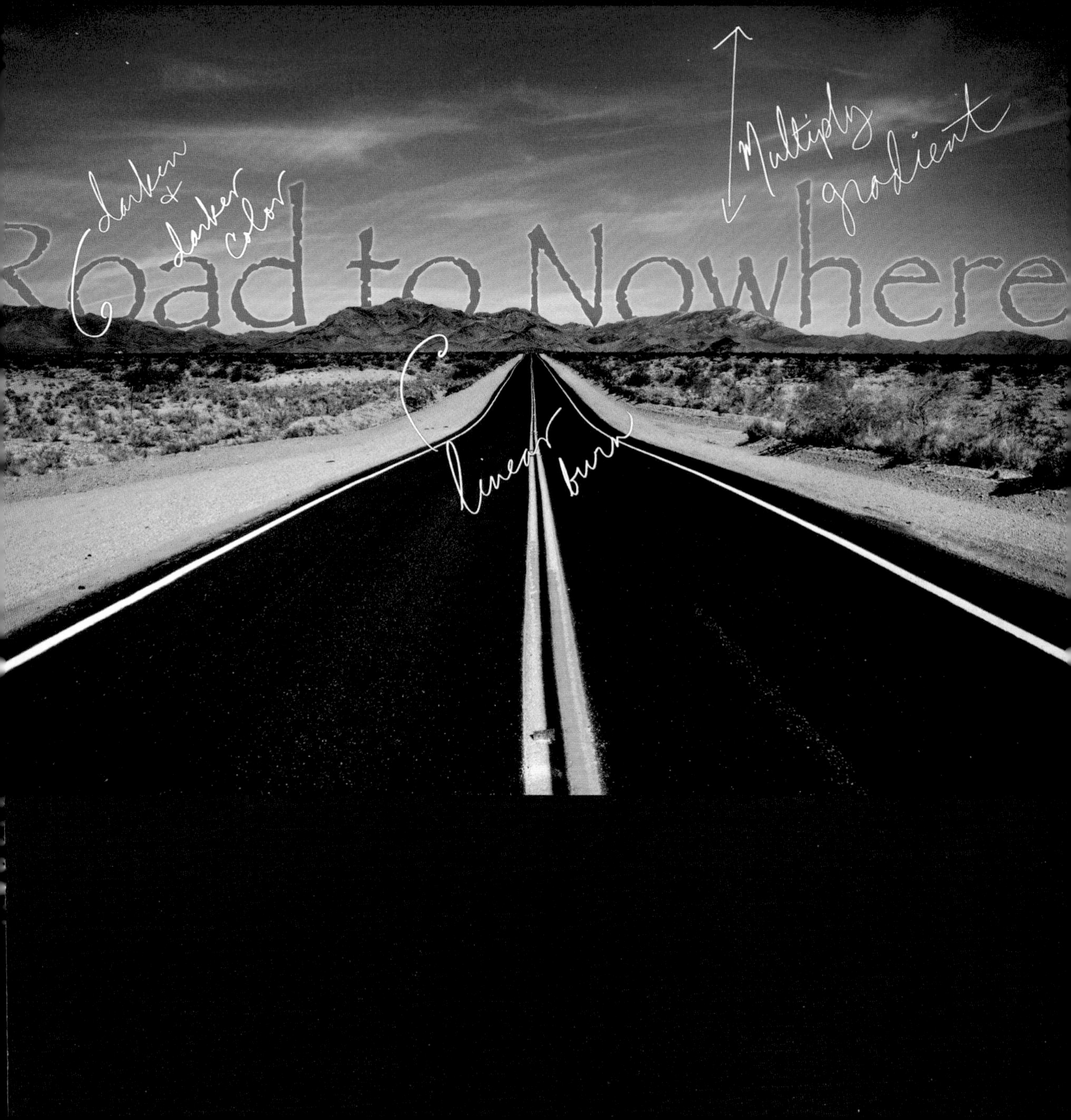

Road to Nowhere

darker &
darker color

Multiply
gradient

linear burn

ALT/OPTION+SHIFT+M

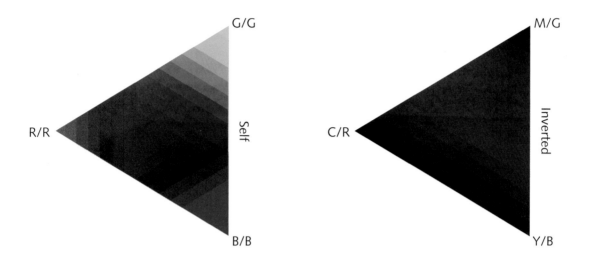

G/G

R/R

Self

B/B

M/G

C/R

Inverted

Y/B

DARKEN, COMMUTATIVE, WHITE

Looks at the color information in each channel and multiplies the base color by the blend color. The result is always a darker color. Multiplying any color by black produces black. Multiplying any color with white leaves the color unchanged. When you're painting with a color other than black or white, successive strokes with a painting tool produce progressively darker colors. The effect is similar to drawing on the image with multiple marking pens.

Output = Base*Blend

Multiply is the default blend mode for the Drop Shadow layer effect, but anything multiplied by black (0,0,0) will stay black. To make more realistic drop shadows, you can select a different color from an area in the image where the shadow will fall.

This mode has no effect on self-blended colors that are already at 100% saturation.

ALT/OPTION+SHIFT+B

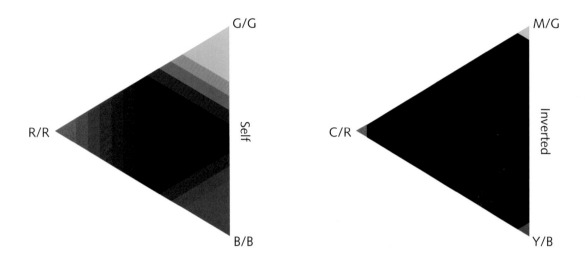

DARKEN, NON-COMMUTATIVE, WHITE

Looks at the color information in each channel and darkens the base color to reflect the blend color by increasing the contrast between the two. Blending with white produces no change.

Output = 1-(1-Base)/Blend

This mode works by dividing the inverse of the base color by the blend color, and then inverting the result. The effect is darker than Multiply, although it still works individually on each channel.

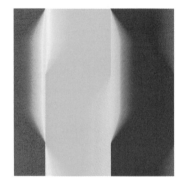

Color Burn behaves differently with fill changes compared to opacity changes. Lowering the fill value removes the effect much more quickly than opacity, giving a subtler and smoother transition between dark and light areas.

Blending with an inverted image results in black, and many middle-value colors will turn black with a self blend. This mode works well with careful masking.

Color Burn is not available in L*a*b space or in 32-bit mode.

ALT/OPTION+SHIFT+A

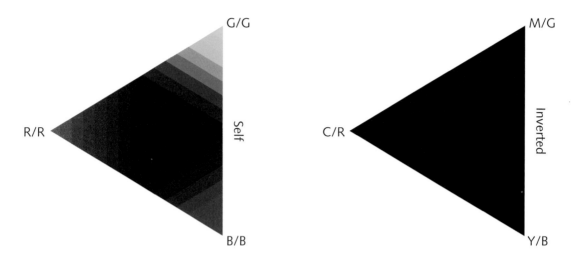

DARKEN, COMMUTATIVE, WHITE

Looks at the color information in each channel and darkens the base color to reflect the blend color by decreasing its brightness. Blending with white produces no change.

Output = (Base+Blend)-1

While still darker than Multiply or Color Burn, Linear Burn is not as saturated as Color Burn. This mode looks like color subtraction and, indeed, white is subtracted from the result of adding the two layers.

Compared to Color Burn, Linear Burn responds with the opposite effect for fill and opacity: Opacity changes are more subtle than fill changes. However, while Color Burn and Linear Burn both give the same results for inverted blends, Linear Burn darkens more colors with self-blends, and produces very different results with complementary blends.

Linear Burn is not available in 32-bit mode.

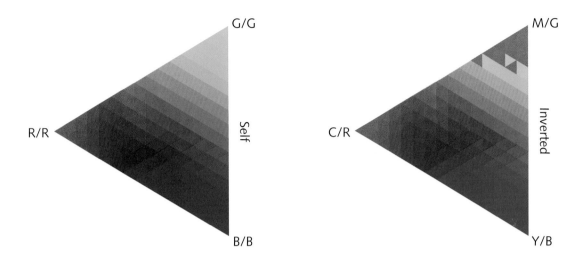

DARKEN, COMMUTATIVE, WHITE

Compares the total of all channel values for the blend and base color and displays the lower value color. Darker Color does not produce a third color, which can result from the Darken blend, because it chooses the lowest channel values from both the base and the blend colors to create the result color.

Output = min(Base, Blend) // Composite operation

This can be a great mode for compositing with subtle textures, especially when combined with Blend If and some masking. Take careful note that this mode operates on the composite channel, so all channel values are combined before the comparison between layers is made. This is how Darker Color avoids generating any intermediate colors.

Darker Color predictably does not affect self-blends, and only partially affects inverse blends. But complementary blends can produce harsh transitions in smooth gradients that involve crossing over 50% gray brightness values.

Darker Color is not available in Grayscale mode.

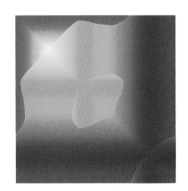

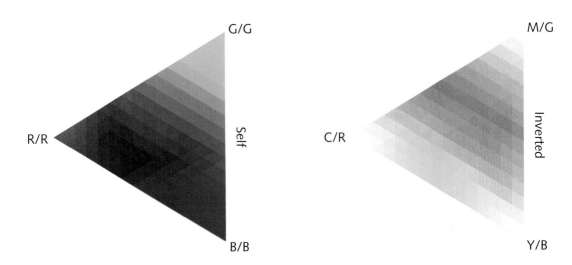

LIGHTEN, COMMUTATIVE, BLACK

Looks at the color information in each channel and selects the base or blend color—whichever is lighter—as the result color. Pixels darker than the blend color are replaced, and pixels lighter than the blend color do not change.

Output = max(Base, Blend) // Channel operation

This is exactly the opposite of Darken, in that the lighter colors are chosen for blending rather than darkening. Again, this operation is performed on each channel independently.

Self-blends produce no change, but inverted blends yield some interesting pastels and soft colors. Painting on a Lighten layer works especially well with soft transitions and edges.

Lighten is not available in L*a*b space.

ALT/OPTION+SHIFT+S

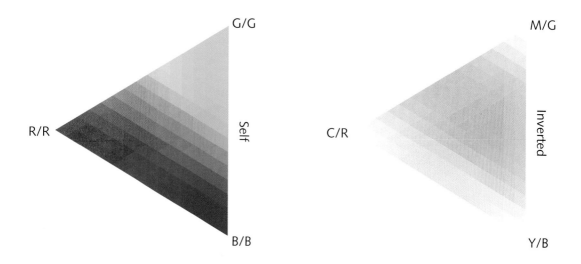

G/G   M/G

R/R   Self   C/R   Inverted

B/B   Y/B

LIGHTEN, COMMUTATIVE, BLACK

Looks at each channel's color information and multiplies the inverse of the blend and base colors. The result color is always a lighter color. Screening with black leaves the color unchanged. Screening with white produces white. The effect is similar to projecting multiple photographic slides on top of each other.

Output = 1-(1-Blend)*(1-Base)

Screen is the opposite of Multiply. It increases brightness by multiplying the inverse of each channel in the blend layer with the inverse of the channels in the base layer, then inverts the result.

This is a great example of "two wrongs don't make a right, but three lefts do."

Screen affects self-blends and can create a soft transition between neighboring colors, though some will tend to blow out to white quickly.

Screen is not available in 32-bit mode.

ALT/OPTION+SHIFT+D

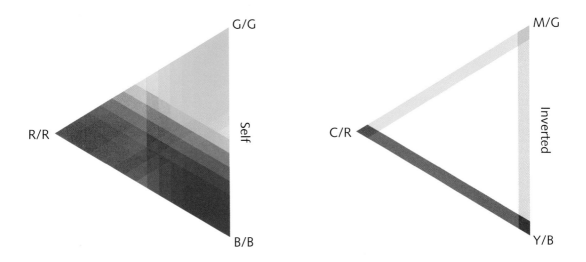

LIGHTEN, NON-COMMUTATIVE, BLACK, FILL

Looks at the color information in each channel and brightens the base color to reflect the blend color by decreasing contrast between the two. Blending with black produces no change.

Output = Base/(1-Blend)

Dodging, if you are not familiar with dark room methods, is a way to brighten image areas during printing of the negative by decreasing exposure selectively, typically using physical methods.

Color Dodge accomplishes this look by dividing the base color by the inverse of the blend color. The result typically has lots of contrast, and most lighter areas are blown out. Using a self-blend produces lots of saturation, while an inverted blend moves everything to white.

Color Dodge is not available in L*a*b space or 32-bit mode.

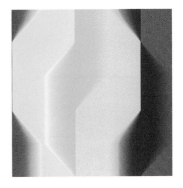

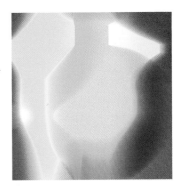

LINEAR DODGE (ADD)

ALT/OPTION+SHIFT+W

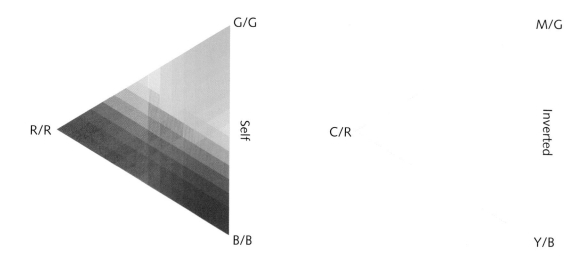

G/G · M/G · R/R · Self · C/R · Inverted · B/B · Y/B

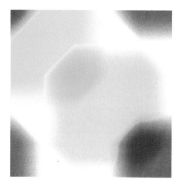

LIGHTEN, COMMUTATIVE, BLACK, FILL

Looks at the color information in each channel and brightens the base color to reflect the blend color by increasing the brightness. Blending with black produces no change.

Output = Base+Blend

This mode is a simple addition of the luminance on each channel. While it can result in blown-out highlights, it's a good mode to start with when you need to uniformly brighten an entire image or selection. Saturation does not go up with this mode as it does with Color Dodge.

Self-blends tend to be brighter than with Color Dodge, but less saturated. Inverted blends still turn solid white.

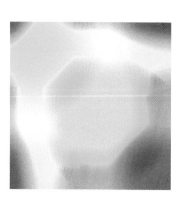

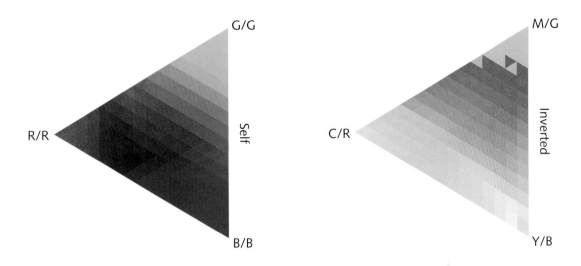

LIGHTEN, COMMUTATIVE, BLACK

Compares the total of all channel values for the blend and base colors and displays the higher value color. Lighter Color does not produce a third color, which can result from the Lighten blend, because it chooses the highest channel values from both the base and blend color to create the result color.

Output = max(Base, Blend) // Composite operation

You might have guessed by now that Lighter Color is the opposite of Darker Color. And just like its counterpart, Lighter Color works on the composite of all the channels. Lighter Color, like all comparison modes, leaves self-blends unchanged. Inverted and complementary blends yield hard transitions across the 50% brightness mark.

Lighter Color is not available in Grayscale mode.

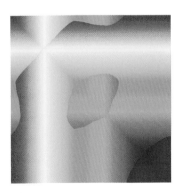

ALT/OPTION+SHIFT+O

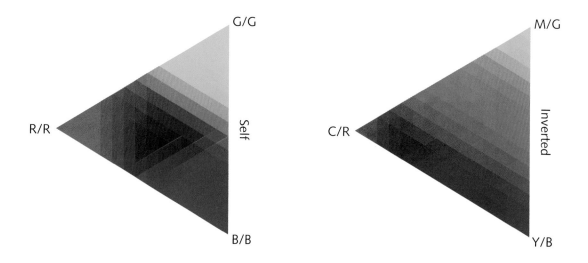

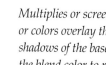

CONTRAST, NON-COMMUTATIVE, 50% GRAY

Multiplies or screens the colors, depending on the base color. Patterns or colors overlay the existing pixels while preserving the highlights and shadows of the base color. The base color is not replaced, but is mixed with the blend color to reflect the lightness or darkness of the original color.

Output = 1-(1-2*(Base-0.5)) * (1-Blend) // For values of Base > 50% (Screen)

Output = (2*Base) × Blend // For values of Base ≤ 50% (Multiply)

Overlay first determines whether a color is brighter or darker than 50% gray, then applies Multiply to darker colors and Screen to lighter. This mode is related to Hard Light in an unusual way. Applying Overlay to the top image gives the same result as if you swapped the layer order and instead applied Hard Light to the top layer (the bottom would now be set to Normal).

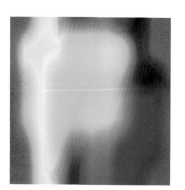

Essentially, Overlay and Hard Light differ by the layer each uses as inputs and outputs. You can see this clearly by comparing the spectrum squares between the two modes.

This mode increases saturation for self-blends, but reduces it for inverted blends.

Overlay is not available in 32-bit mode.

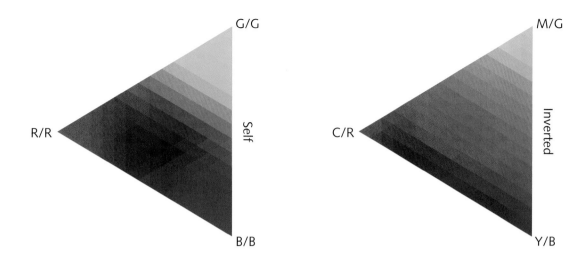

CONTRAST, NON-COMMUTATIVE, 50% GRAY

Darkens or lightens the colors, depending on the blend color. The resulting effect is similar to shining a diffused spotlight on the image. If the blend color (light source) is lighter than 50% gray, the image is lightened as if it were dodged. If the blend color is darker than 50% gray, the image is darkened as if it were burned in. Painting with pure black or white produces a distinctly darker or lighter area, but does not result in pure black or white.

Output = 1-(1-Base)*(1-(Blend-0.5)) // For values of Blend > 50% (Dodge)

Output = Base*(Blend+0.5) // For values of Blend ≤ 50% (Burn)

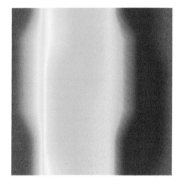

Soft Light behaves similarly to Overlay, but with less contrast. The end result produces softer transitions across brightness and colors, and what appears to be translucent blending in shadows and highlights.

Soft Light is not available in 32-bit mode.

ALT/OPTION+SHIFT+H

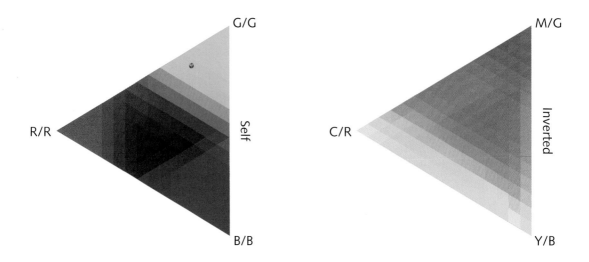

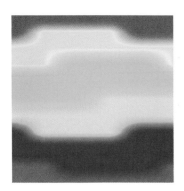

CONTRAST, NON-COMMUTATIVE, 50% GRAY

Multiplies or screens the colors, depending on the blend color. The effect is similar to shining a harsh spotlight on the image. If the blend color (light source) is lighter than 50% gray, the image is lightened, as if it were screened. This is useful for adding highlights to an image. If the blend color is darker than 50% gray, the image is darkened, as if it were multiplied. This is useful for adding shadows to an image. Painting with pure black or white results in pure black or white.

Output = 1-(1-Base)*(1-2*(Blend-0.5)) // For values of Blend > 50% (Screen)

Output = Base*(2*Blend) // For values of Blend ≤ 50% (Multiply)

Hard Light is really a combination of Multiply and Screen split at the 50% gray level. As noted previously, it's related to Overlay.

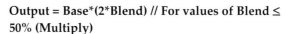

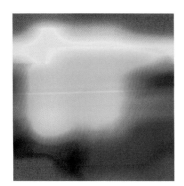

When applied to a self-blend, contrast is increased and middle tones become black. But for an inverted blend, the result is brighter and less saturated than Soft Light.

Hard Light is not available in 32-bit mode.

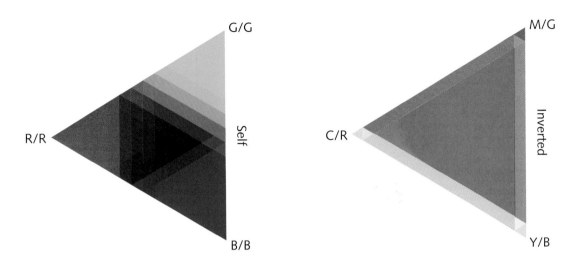

CONTRAST, NON-COMMUTATIVE, 50% GRAY, FILL

Burns or dodges the colors by increasing or decreasing the contrast, depending on the blend color. If the blend color (light source) is lighter than 50% gray, the image is lightened by decreasing the contrast. If the blend color is darker than 50% gray, the image is darkened by increasing the contrast.

Output = 1-(1-Base)/(2*(Blend-0.5)) // For values of Blend > 50% (Color Burn)

Output = Base/(1-2*Blend) // For values of Blend ≤ 50% (Color Dodge)

Vivid Light pushes contrast to the point of full saturation in self-blends, but results in 50% gray. Notice that the self-blend triangle very quickly goes from black to full saturation. It accomplishes this by applying Color Dodge to the lighter pixels and Color Burn to the darker ones.

Fill and Opacity changes behave differently with this mode.

Vivid Light is not available in 32-bit mode.

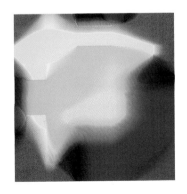

ALT/OPTION+SHIFT+J

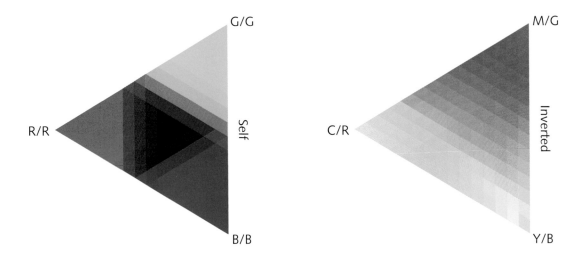

CONTRAST, NON-COMMUTATIVE, 50% GRAY, FILL

Burns or dodges the colors by decreasing or increasing the brightness, depending on the blend color. If the blend color (light source) is lighter than 50% gray, the image is lightened by increasing the brightness. If the blend color is darker than 50% gray, the image is darkened by decreasing the brightness.

Output = Base+2*(Blend-0.5) // For values of Blend > 50% (Linear Dodge)

Ouput = Base+2*Blend-1 // For values of Blend ≤ 50% (Linear Burn)

This mode uses Linear Burn and Linear Dodge in much the same way that Vivid Light uses the Color versions. Interestingly, this results in inverted blends that create complementary colors, while the self-blend has even more contrast than Vivid Light.

Linear Light is not available in 32-bit mode.

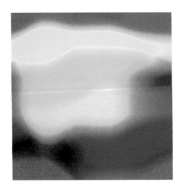

ALT/OPTION+SHIFT+Z

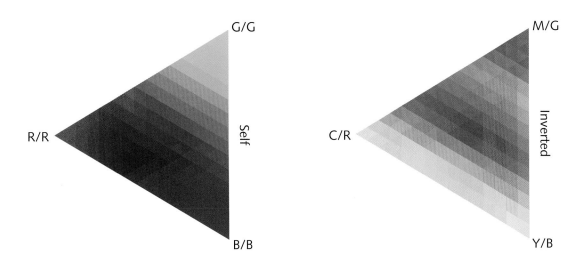

G/G

R/R

Self

B/B

M/G

C/R

Inverted

Y/B

CONTRAST, NON-COMMUTATIVE, 50% GRAY

Replaces the colors, depending on the blend color. If the blend color (light source) is lighter than 50% gray, pixels darker than the blend color are replaced, and pixels lighter than the blend color do not change. If the blend color is darker than 50% gray, pixels lighter than the blend color are replaced, and pixels darker than the blend color do not change. This is useful for adding special effects to an image.

Output = max(Base, 2*(Blend-0.5)) // For values of Blend > 50%

Output = min(Base, 2*Blend) // For values of Blend ≤ 50%

Pin Light can result in different, incongruous areas of color. To best understand this, look at the inverted blend triangle. Note that the overall brightness is relatively stable, while there are odd sections of slightly unexpected colors.

Even more interesting is the regular patterns that show up in the spectrum squares. This is one way you can see that the CMY colors have different definitions of brightness than RGB.

Pin Light is not available in 32-bit mode.

ALT/OPTION+SHIFT+L

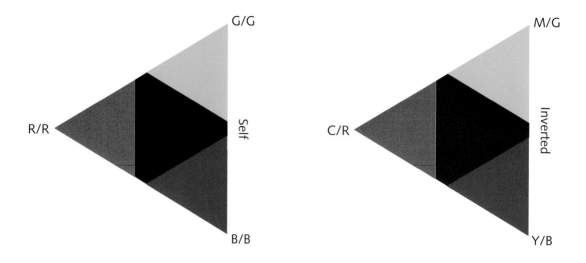

CONTRAST, COMMUTATIVE, 50% GRAY, FILL

Adds the red, green, and blue channel values of the blend color to the RGB values of the base color. If the resulting sum for a channel is 255 or greater, it receives a value of 255; if less than 255, a value of 0. Therefore, all blended pixels have red, green, and blue channel values of either 0 or 255. This changes all pixels to primary additive colors (red, green, or blue), white, or black.

Output = 255 for Base+Blend ≤ 255

Output = 0 for Base+Blend < 255

For CMYK images, Hard Mix changes all pixels to the primary subtractive colors (cyan, yellow, or magenta), white, or black. The maximum color value is 100.

Hard Mix is a weird mode, indeed. It operates on each channel individually and pushes the normally gray values to pure black or white. That results in a total of eight possible colors (RGB, CMY) plus black and white.

Taking things a bit further, Hard Mix also responds differently to Fill and Opacity. Start by changing fill when you want to smoothly blend the result into your base and retain some of the detail of the base. It's also one of my favorite modes for developing geometric patterns and textures.

Hard Mix is not available in 32-bit mode.

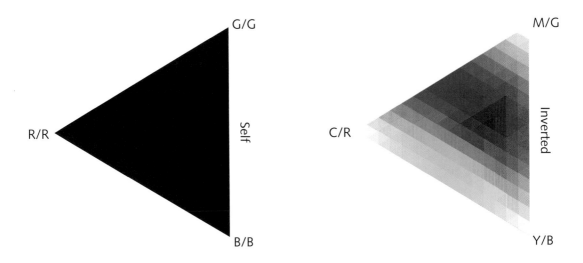

COMPARISON, COMMUTATIVE, BLACK

Looks at the color information in each channel and subtracts either the blend color from the base color or the base color from the blend color, depending on which has the greater brightness value. Blending with white inverts the base color values; blending with black produces no change.

Output = abs(Base-Blend)

If you read that carefully, you'll see that the Difference mode is really doing a simple subtraction, but keeps the result as an absolute value—the output can never be negative, which wouldn't make sense anyway. Self-blends result in black, but most other blends generate new colors.

Difference Mode is used to great effect when comparing or aligning image layers. It responds differently to Opacity and Fill.

Difference is not available in L*a*b space.

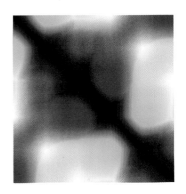

ALT/OPTION+SHIFT+X

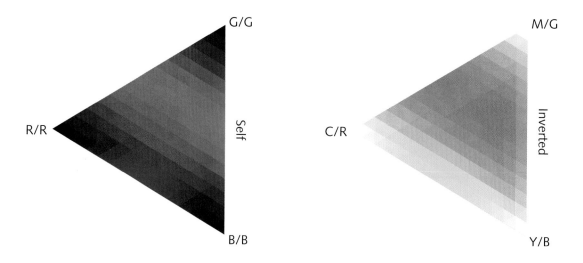

G/G

R/R

Self

B/B

M/G

C/R

Inverted

Y/B

COMPARISON, COMMUTATIVE, BLACK

Creates an effect similar to but lower in contrast than the Difference mode. Blending with white inverts the base color values. Blending with black produces no change.

Output = Blend+Base-2*Base*Blend

Self-blends produce a very desaturated, but not gray result with colors similar to those produced by Difference mode. Inverted blends look similar to Hard Light, but the differences in brightness calculations can yield different colors.

Exclusion is not available in L*a*b space or 32-bit mode.

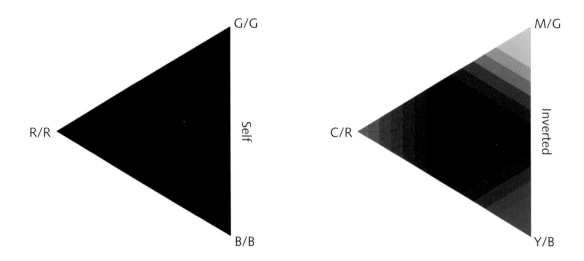

COMPARISON, NON-COMMUTATIVE, BLACK

Looks at the color information in each channel and subtracts the blend color from the base color. In 8- and 16-bit images, any resulting negative values are clipped to zero.

Output = Base-Blend

There's not much more to say about this blend mode. It does what it says, and can easily result in lots of black areas. Self-blends turn out solid black, while inverted blends can be black or nearly fully saturated.

Subtract is not available in L*a*b space.

NO KEYBOARD SHORTCUT

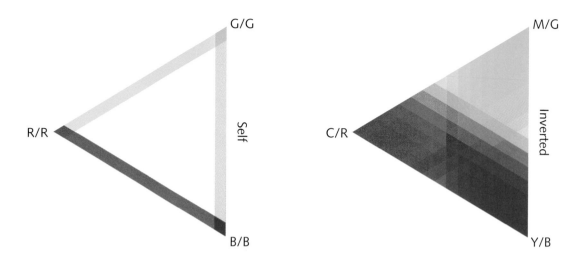

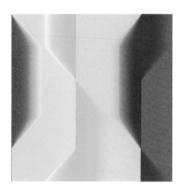

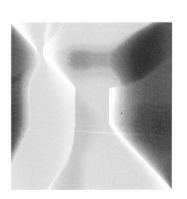

COMPARISON, NON-COMMUTATIVE, BLACK

Looks at the color information in each channel and divides the blend color from the base color.

Output = Blend/Base

Divide is easier to understand when you remember that the channel gray values are normalized or converted to a percentage. Self-blends result in solid white because any number divided by itself is 1, or 100%. Similarly, blending with black (0%) gives you black. This mode is identical to inverting the top image and setting the blend mode to Color Dodge.

While this mode has creative uses, Divide is mainly intended for use with calibrated technical images, such as those found in astrophotography and microscopy.

Dividing by zero in this case does not cause Photoshop to implode or even hiccup. So your plans for world domination won't find outlet here.

Divide is not available in L*a*b space.

ALT/OPTION+SHIFT+U

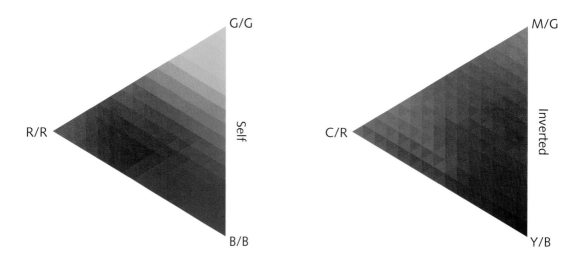

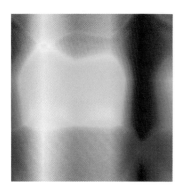

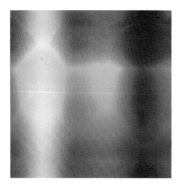

COMPOSITE, NON-COMMUTATIVE, NONE

Creates a result color with the luminance and saturation of the base color and the hue of the blend color.

The key to Hue is that it considers only the saturation of the base color in its calculation. When a base color is neutral gray, it will not apply hue at all, which makes it similar to Saturation mode. This is different than Color, which applies the blend color regardless of saturation in the base.

Hue is not available in Grayscale mode.

ALT/OPTION+SHIFT+T

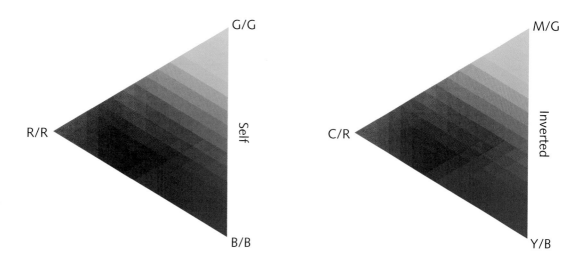

COMPOSITE, NON-COMMUTATIVE, NONE

Creates a result color with the luminance and hue of the base color and the saturation of the blend color. Painting with this mode in an area with no (0) saturation (gray) causes no change.

This blend mode is useful for matching saturation when hue and luminance are already dialed in.

Saturation is not available in Grayscale mode.

ALT/OPTION+SHIFT+C

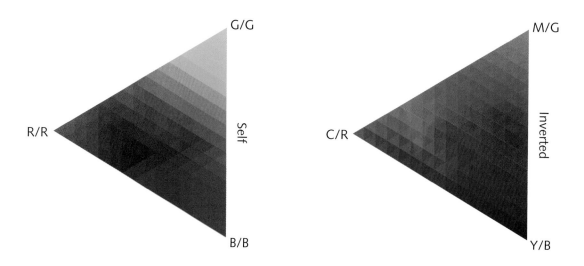

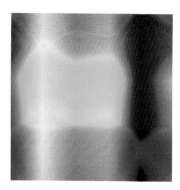

COMPOSITE, NON-COMMUTATIVE, NONE

Creates a result color with the luminance of the base color and the hue and saturation of the blend color. This preserves the gray levels in the image and is useful for coloring monochrome images and for tinting color images.

Color is a favorite of photo restorers because it doesn't affect the apparent brightness of an image. The result can be quite natural when handled carefully. It is related to Luminosity in the same way that Overlay is to Hard Light; that is, applying Color to the top layer gives the same output as if you applied Luminosity to the bottom layer, then swapped the stacking order and changed the base to Normal.

Self-blends have no effect, but inverse blends are somewhat muted and result in new colors.

Color is not available in Grayscale mode.

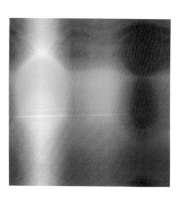

ALT/OPTION+SHIFT+Y

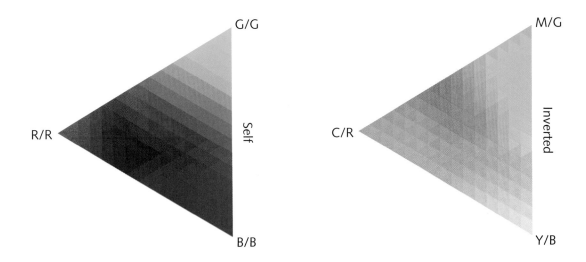

COMPOSITE, NON-COMMUTATIVE, NONE

Creates a result color with the hue and saturation of the base color and the luminance of the blend color. This mode creates the inverse effect of Color mode.

Again, self-blends have no effect, but inverted blends yield some nice pastels with increased brightness. Luminosity is also used in several techniques to keep colors from shifting when an adjustment is made.

Luminosity is not available in Grayscale mode.

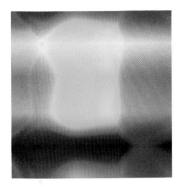

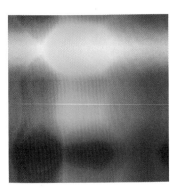

Some other blend modes appear in odd places, such as tool options and layer styles. Some are unexpectedly useful, while others are decidedly not so useful. All of these additional modes are not explained in full here; but, in any case, you can best understand them by trying them out. I've yet to find a good use for some (such as Multiply in the Spot Healing brush) when using a standard workflow.

If you have found an application for these variations, I'd love to hear about it.

PASS THROUGH

COMPOSITE, VARIES, VARIES

By default, the blending mode of a layer group is Pass Through, which means that the group has no blending properties of its own. When you choose a different blending mode for a group, you effectively change the order in which the image components are put together. First, all of the layers in the group are put together. The composite group is then treated as a single image and blended with the rest of the image using the selected blending mode. Therefore, if you choose a blending mode other than Pass Through for the group, none of the adjustment layers or layer blending modes inside the group will apply to layers outside the group.

For example, in a document with two layers, setting the blend mode of the top layer behaves as expected, and gives a result that combines the two layers. Putting the top layer into a group by itself set to Pass Through does not change the output. But setting the group's mode to Normal causes the top layer's blend mode to affect only other layers in the group, so no blending occurs between the group and the layer beneath. Likewise, using any other Group blend mode treats the contents of that group as if they were already combined.

Pass Through is available only to groups, but can be applied to nested groups. If you are mathematically inclined, think of groups as parentheses around parts of an equation. Pass Through removes the parentheses, while other blend modes create a function out of the group.

TOOL BLEND MODES

Many tools in Photoshop use blend modes, though some uses are less obvious than others. Layer Effects are not included in this list because they are accessed directly from the Layers panel and include all the same modes. The core layer blend modes are those already listed, while additional modes are included under each tool.

Some modes are accessible only when certain options are selected, and others may appear to have no real function at all. Pay close attention to tool-specific blend modes and be sure to tinker with them to understand how they work.

BRUSH

The paint brush, when active, has all of the core layer blend modes available to it, and adds two:

BEHIND

ALT/OPTION+SHIFT+Q

Edits or paints only on the transparent part of a layer. This mode works only on layers with Lock Transparency deselected and is analogous to painting on the back of transparent areas of a sheet of acetate. While it may first appear to be of limited utility, it can be a great way to add a few extra pixels to images in which mask has already been applied.

You can achieve a similar effect by painting on a layer beneath the target layer, then merging them.

CLEAR

ALT/OPTION+SHIFT+R

Edits or paints each pixel and makes it transparent. This mode is available for the Shape tools (when Fill Pixels is selected), Paint Bucket tool, Brush tool, Pencil tool, Fill command, and Stroke command. You must be on an unlocked layer and with Lock Transparency deselected to use this mode.

This functions exactly the same as the Eraser tool.

BRUSH SETTINGS

If that weren't enough, the brush settings panel allows you to blend textures and other markers using the blend modes listed here. Of these, there are two new modes: Linear Height and Height.

These blend modes work on gray scale only and act to invert the texture chosen in the Brushes panel, but otherwise use the same rules noted in the standard modes previously listed. I have not included descriptions on each of these because they are best understood by using them. Counter to the advice I gave about predicting blend mode results, these modes are easier to just experiment with.

TEXTURE

Multiply, Subtract, Darken, Overlay, Color Dodge, Color Burn, Linear Burn, Hard Mix, Linear Height, Height

DUAL BRUSH

Multiply, Darken, Overlay, Color Dodge, Color Burn, Linear Burn, Hard Mix, Linear Height

SPOT HEALING BRUSH & HEALING BRUSH

Normal, Replace, Multiply, Screen, Darken, Lighten, Color, Luminosity

COLOR REPLACEMENT

Hue, Saturation, Color, Luminosity

CLONE STAMP, PATTERN STAMP, HISTORY BRUSH, GRADIENT, PAINT BUCKET

Same as Brush, but excludes Clear

ART HISTORY, BLUR, SHARPEN, SMUDGE TOOLS

Normal, Darken, Lighten, Hue, Saturation, Color, Luminosity

DODGE, BURN

Shadows, Midtones, Highlights

SPONGE

Desaturate, Saturate

SHAPE TOOL

All core layer modes when using the Pixels option

FADE

All core layer modes

CALCULATIONS, APPLY IMAGE

All layer modes, plus Add, but excludes: Dissolve; Hue; Saturation; Color; Luminosity

PART IV
APPENDICES

A collection of additional information relating to blend modes, including quick reference materials, recommended reading, and details of color spaces and bit depths.

COLOR MODES AND BIT DEPTH

A short explanation why and when some blend modes are not available in Photoshop.

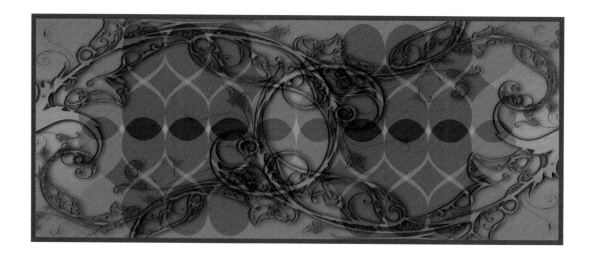

The blend modes in Photoshop were generally written for 8-bit operation in the RGB color space. As a result, several of them do not work in other color spaces or at higher bit depths. Refer to the PDF specification, ISO 32000-1, to see the complete publicly available blend mode calculations.

Of particular note are the limitations on 32-bit depth, which is used for High Dynamic Range (HDR) images. These are typically composite images made up of very large ranges of brightness. 32-bit mode precludes some blending modes because it runs its numerical model from negative to positive infinity. Because 8-bit and 16-bit images use only positive integers only, much of the blending math would not be meaningful (or even possible) given the intent of 32-bit mode.

32-bit mode is also not available in CMYK or L*a*b color spaces. To take advantage of 32-bit images, you will need to develop a work flow that includes converting to 16-bit or 8-bit. This can typically be accomplished near the end of the editing process as most output devices require conversion to 16-bit depth or lower.

L*a*b space is also limited due to the way its channels are built. Trying to convert to L*a*b from another space will return any disallowed modes to Normal blending, so you must first "commit" these modes by flattening your image or merging. If you choose to flatten your image, I highly recommend that you first make a copy to convert, and save your original.

In general, it's a good idea to use a flattened copy of your image to perform conversions between bit depths and color spaces, preserving your original for later corrections or changes.

For 3D images, especially textures and depth maps, higher bit depth is usully desirable. In fact, rendering in 32-bit color space is much faster than in other bit depths. And in grayscale depth maps and bump maps, 16-bit yields much smoother gradients and transitions. That's because you have more levels of gray to work with, so each "step" between shades is much smaller. In this case, consider making your 3D file 32-bit, with at least 16-bit bump and depth maps, and then render the image by itself. Once you have your complete 3D render, save the render out to a new file and convert down to 16-bit for blend mode operations.

APPENDIX B
BLEND MODES REFERENCE TABLE

The following table summarizes important information about blend modes in Photoshop. You'll find shortcuts, neutral colors, and available bit depths and color space listed for each blend mode.

The Exclusions entry shows where a mode is not available. Blend modes are unavailable in Multichannel mode.

NORMAL

NORMAL (CMD/CTRL + SHIFT + N)

Neutral Color:
None

Exclusions:
None

DISSOLVE (NONE)

Neutral Color:
None

Exclusions:
None

DARKEN

DARKEN (CMD/CTRL + SHIFT + K)

Neutral Color:
White

Exclusions:
L*a*b

MULTIPLY (CMD/CTRL + SHIFT + M)

Neutral Color:
White

Exclusions:
None

COLOR BURN (CMD/CTRL + SHIFT + B)

Neutral Color:
White

Exclusions:
L*a*b, 32-bit

LINEAR BURN (CMD/CTRL + SHIFT + A)

Neutral Color:
White

Exclusions:
32-bit

DARKER COLOR (NONE)

Neutral Color:
White

Exclusions:
Grayscale

LIGHTEN

LIGHTEN (CMD/CTRL + SHIFT + G)

Neutral Color:
Black

Exclusions:
L*a*b

SCREEN (CMD/CTRL + SHIFT + S)

Neutral Color:
Black

Exclusions:
32-bit

COLOR DODGE (CMD/CTRL + SHIFT + D)

Neutral Color:
Black

Exclusions:
32-bit, L*a*b

LINEAR DODGE (CMD/CTRL + SHIFT + W)

Neutral Color:
Black

Exclusions:
None

LIGHTER COLOR (NONE)

Neutral Color:
Black

Exclusions:
Grayscale

OVERLAY (CMD/CTRL + SHIFT + O)

Neutral Color:
50% Gray

Exclusions:
32-bit

SOFT LIGHT (CMD/CTRL + SHIFT + F)

Neutral Color:
50% Gray

Exclusions:
32-bit

HARD LIGHT (CMD/CTRL + SHIFT + H)

Neutral Color:
50% Gray

Exclusions:
32-bit

VIVID LIGHT (CMD/CTRL + SHIFT + V)

Neutral Color:
50% Gray

Exclusions:
32-bit

LINEAR LIGHT (CMD/CTRL + SHIFT + J)

Neutral Color:
50% Gray

Exclusions:
32-bit

PIN LIGHT (CMD/CTRL + SHIFT + Z)

Neutral Color:
50% Gray

Exclusions:
32-bit

HARD MIX (CMD/CTRL + SHIFT + L)

Neutral Color:
50% Gray

Exclusions:
32-bit

COMPARE

DIFFERENCE (CMD/CTRL + SHIFT + E)

Neutral Color:
Black

Exclusions:
L*a*b

EXCLUSION (CMD/CTRL + SHIFT + X)

Neutral Color:
Black

Exclusions:
L*a*b, 32-bit

SUBTRACT (NONE)

Neutral Color:
Black

Exclusions:
L*a*b

DIVIDE (NONE)

Neutral Color:
Black

Exclusions:
L*a*b

COMPOSITE (HSL)

HUE (CMD/CTRL + SHIFT + U)

Neutral Color:
None

Exclusions:
Grayscale

SATURATION (CMD/CTRL + SHIFT + T)

Neutral Color:
None

Exclusions:
Grayscale

COLOR (CMD/CTRL + SHIFT + C)

Neutral Color:
None

Exclusions:
Grayscale

LUMINOSITY (CMD/CTRL + SHIFT + Y)

Neutral Color:
None

Exclusions:
Grayscale

APPENDIX C
ONLINE RESOURCES

Many additional resources are available online, but I find that those listed here have something special to offer. I've also included my own site, which has some sample PSD files from the Blend Modes in Depth section, along with various actions and other useful Photoshop tidbits.

I first want to showcase two tools that became available just as this book was going to print. The first is Dr. Russell Brown's Texture panel for Photoshop CS6. This handy extension lets you cycle through textures and blend modes rapidly, choosing from a specific folder with texture images. It's a great way to try out several options very quickly before deciding on the right look for your picture. You'll find the link in the table below.

The second is Chuck Uebele's Scripted Fill User Interface. New to Photoshop CS6, the Scripted Fill feature lets you specify a target and source image, along with a defined pattern to fill a selected area. Chuck's script gives this feature a user interface with access to many of its capabilities, including blend modes. Don't miss this one!

Finally, you'll find a recap of the websites run by the talented and generous guest authors who contributed recipes to this book.

Table C.1 Recommended Websites

SITE NAME	BRIEF DESCRIPTION	URL
Scott Valentine	Additions to this book	lightningsymphony.com/hpobm or scoxel.com/hpobm
Russell Brown	Texture panel for CS6	russellbrown.com/texturespotlight.html
Chuck Uebele	Scripted fill user interface	uebelephoto.com/CS6_Fill.html
Adobe	PDF specification (technical basis for blend modes)	adobe.com/content/dam/Adobe/en/devnet/acrobat/pdfs/PDF32000_2008.pdf
M2 Media Studios	Online courses and learning materials	m2media.com

Table C.2 Websites of Guest Authors

SITE NAME	URL
Carrie Beene	carrienyc.com
Steve Caplin	howtocheatinphotoshop.com
RC Concepcion	aboutrc.com
Katrin Eismann	katrineismann.com
Chris Georgenes	mudbubble.com
Kat Gilbert	inthewoodonline.com
Mark Heaps	markheaps.com
Calvin Hollywood	calvinhollywood.de
Matt Kloskowski	mattkloskowski.com
Julieanne Kost	jkost.com
Patrick LaMontagne	cartoonink.com
John Shannon	jeshannon.com
Chris Tarantino	christarantino.com
Jim Tierney	digitalanarchy.com

BLEND MODE TOOLS MATRIX

Blend modes are found throughout Photoshop. The following table lists the blend modes and the tools that can use them.

BLEND MODES	Layers	Layer Styles	Spot Healing Brush	Healing Brush	Clone & Pattern Stamps	Brush & Pencil	Brush Settings—Texture
Normal	x	x	x	x	x	x	
Dissolve	x	x			x	x	
Darken	x	x	x	x	x	x	x
Multiply	x	x	x	x	x	x	x
Color Burn	x	x			x	x	x
Linear Burn	x	x			x	x	x
Darker Color	x	x			x	x	
Lighten	x	x	x	x	x	x	
Screen	x	x	x	x	x	x	
Color Dodge	x	x			x	x	x
Linear Dodge	x	x			x	x	
Lighter Color	x	x			x	x	
Overlay	x	x			x	x	x
Soft Light	x	x			x	x	
Hard Light	x	x			x	x	
Vivid Light	x	x			x	x	
Linear Light	x	x			x	x	
Pin Light	x	x			x	x	
Hard Mix	x	x			x	x	x
Difference	x	x			x	x	
Exclusion	x	x			x	x	
Subtract	x	x			x	x	x
Divide	x	x			x	x	
Hue	x	x			x	x	
Saturation	x	x			x	x	
Color	x	x	x	x	x	x	
Luminosity	x	x	x	x	x	x	
Clear						x	
Behind					x	x	
Height							x
Linear Height							x

BLEND MODES	TOOLS						
	Brush Settings—Dual Brush	Color Replacement	History Brush	Art History Brush	Gradient	Paint Bucket	Blur, Sharpen, Smudge
Normal			x	x	x	x	x
Dissolve			x		x	x	
Darken	x		x	x	x	x	x
Multiply	x		x		x	x	
Color Burn	x		x		x	x	
Linear Burn	x		x		x	x	
Darker Color			x		x	x	
Lighten			x	x	x	x	x
Screen			x		x	x	
Color Dodge	x		x		x	x	
Linear Dodge			x		x	x	
Lighter Color			x		x	x	
Overlay	x		x		x	x	
Soft Light			x		x	x	
Hard Light			x		x	x	
Vivid Light			x		x	x	
Linear Light			x		x	x	
Pin Light			x		x	x	
Hard Mix	x		x		x	x	
Difference			x		x	x	
Exclusion			x		x	x	
Subtract	x		x		x	x	
Divide			x		x	x	
Hue		x	x	x	x	x	x
Saturation		x	x	x	x	x	x
Color		x	x	x	x	x	x
Luminosity		x	x	x	x	x	x
Clear						x	
Behind			x		x	x	
Height							x
Linear Height	x						x

INDEX

NUMBERS

3D images
    blend modes in   103–104
    depth maps applied to   112–114
    texture maps applied to   122–123
8-bit images   140
16-bit images   139, 140
32-bit images   140

A

accuracy, digital tablets and   9–10
Add Layer Mask button, for pixelated
    edges   86–87
Adjustment blend   15
adjustment layer(s). *See also specific adjustment*
    layers
    with blend modes   15
    file size and   7
    noise   81
Advanced Blending dialog box
    gentle rain technique and   95
    for glowing dust effect   119–121
    for soft-glow effect   78–79
    trapping transparency   80
alpha channel   19
Ansel Adams 10-Zone System   56
Apply Image tool
    blend modes with   179
    features of   25–26
Art History brush setting   178
astrophotography, Divide mode for   170
Average Blur filter   38

B

background color, removing vignettes and
    49–50
background knowledge   8–9

background layer
    channel selections from   51–53
    duplicating blurred   82–83
    duplicating twice   98–99
    duplicating/converting to SO   58–59,
        86–87
    duplicating/inverting   74–75
    duplicating/setting to Hard Mix   90
    self-blend   15
Basic self-blend   15
Beene, Carrie   89
Behind blend mode
    with custom brushes   107
    features/functions of   177
    for illustration shading   126
bit depth   139, 140
Black & White adjustment layer
    for hand-tinted look   71
    in Hard Mix Noise technique   93
    Luminosity mode and   43–44
    noise with   81
black color
    creating vignettes   54–55
    in custom lens flair effect   88–89
    to darken images   40
    Divide mode and   170
    Multiply mode and   150
    in self-blends   167
    Subtract mode and   169
blank layers
    hand-tinted look and   71
    merging with rain layer   95
Blend If tool
    adjusting transparency with   16
    blending layers   23–24
    increasing contrast and   90
    removing vignettes and   50
blend mode(s). *See also specific blend modes*
    bit depth and   140
    combining   16–19
    experience with   10

features of 5–7, 14
general groups 138
layer groups and 98–99
listings, understanding of 138
mathematics of 139
most needed 37
painting with 19–22
reference images for 27–30
sharpening images with 60–62
for tools 177
Blur brush setting 178
blurring. *See also* Gaussian blur
color highlights and 109
in combined blends 16, 18
brightness
adjusting with gradients 56–57
Color Dodge mode and 157
Curves adjustments for 63
enhancing eyes 39
Linear Dodge mode and 158
Brightness/Contrast adjustment layer 81
Brush Presets panel 106–107, 178–179
Brush Tip Shape tab 107
Brush tool
blend modes for 19–22, 177–179
custom brushes and 105–107
for illustration shading 124–126
set to Difference mode 122–123
brush, small scatter 119–121
Burn tool
blend modes with 178
destructive blending with 14

C

Calculations tool
blend modes with 179
channel blending and 25–26, 51–53
Camera Raw plug-in 49–50
Caplin, Steve 127
cartoons, Soft Light mode for 133
center point, 8-bit image 140

channel blending, Calculations and 25–26, 51–53
Channels panel 51–53
checkerboard patterns 128
classic illustration shading 124–126
Claw key method 18, 19
Clear blend mode
custom brushes and 107
features/functions of 177
clipping layers
function of 15
for underexposure recovery 46
Clone Stamp brush setting 20–22, 178
CMYK color model
Hard Mix mode and 166
reference images in 27
Color Balance adjustment layer 127
Color blend mode
for 3D images 104
features/functions of 7, 174
gray layer and 70
hand-tinted look with 71
for illustrations 109
monochrome look with 70
Color Burn blend mode
features/functions of 151
illustrated textures with 116–118
underexposure recovery and 46
color cast removal 38
Color Dodge blend mode
color illustrations and 108–111
custom lens flair effect with 88–89
features/functions of 157
Color Dynamics option 107
color filters 5–6
Color Replacement brush setting 178
color(s)
blend modes adding 66–67
comparisons, global 27–28
highlights 108–111

color(s) (*continued*)
   inversion   141
   neutral   138
   new, Darken mode and   148
   primary subtractive   166
   replacing   165
Colorize option
   checkerboard patterns and   128
   portraits and   69
combining blends   16–19
committing blends   18
Commutative label   138
comparison blend modes   159
complementary blends, with Darker Color
   mode   153
compositing
   with Darker Color mode   153
   with Lighter Color mode   159
Concepcion, RC   76
continuous spectrum image   28–29
Contour setting, for glowing dust effect
   119–121
contrast
   Color Dodge mode and   157
   Hard Mix mode and   90
   in portraits   68–69
   Vivid Light mode and   163
Create New Channel icon   86–87
Create New Layer icon   88–89
Crosshatch filter   72–75
crosshatch textures   130
Curves adjustment layer
   applying luminosity to   15
   saturation/luminosity with   63
   underexposure recovery and   46
custom brushes   105–107
custom lens flair/glow effect   88–89

D

Darken blend mode   148
Darker Color blend mode   153

depth maps, in 3D modeling   112–114
destructiveness
   of Dodge and Burn   40
   of painting tools   14
Details, Freaky   98–99
Difference blend mode
   Brush tool set to   20, 122–123
   edge contrast and   45
   features/functions of   167
   Gradient tool set to   115
digital tablets   9–10, 40
Dissolve blend mode
   adjustment layer noise and   81
   Brush tool set to   20
   features/functions of   147
   illustration shading with   124–126
   pixelated edges with   86–87
   soft brush set to   106
Distance setting, for glowing dust effect
   119–121
Divide blend mode
   combining blends and   19
   edge contrast with   45
   features/functions of   170
   graphic illustrations with   82–83
   illustrated textures with   116–118
   line sketches and   72–73
   removing vignettes and   49–50
   texture with   76–77
Dodge and Burn tool   40–42
   adding shading   127
   glowing dust effect and   119–121
   Orton effect and   16–17
Dodge tool
   blend modes with   178
   destructive blending and   14
dodging technique   157
dot size, in illustration shading   126
Drop Shadow effect
   for edges   80
   for glowing lines/dust   119–121

Layer Style dialog box and   24–25
  Multiply mode for   150
Dual Brush setting   107, 178
Dust trail, glowing lines and   119–121

E

edges
  Drop Shadow effect   80
  increasing contrast on   45
  by merging layers   18
  pixelated   86–87
Eismann, Katrin   60
Elliptical Marquee tool, to lighten eyes   39
Eraser tool, for color illustrations   109
ergonomics, digital tablets and   9–10
Exclusion blend mode
  features/functions of   168
  overlapping strokes and   21
Eyedropper tool, in removing vignettes   49–50
eyes, lightening of   39

F

fabric textures   130
Fade command
  blending layers with   22–23
  crosshatch textures with   130
Fade Filter option   16
Fade tool   179
Fibers filter, in gentle rain technique   94–97
file size, adjustment layers and   7
Fill label, on blend mode listing   138
Fill option
  blend technique   15
  blending layers with   22
  isolating layer styles with   25
Fill values
  Color Burn mode and   151
  Hard Mix mode and   166
  Hard Mix Noise technique and   93
Filtered self-blend   15

filters
  Average Blur   38
  changing blend mode of   27
  color   5–6
  Crosshatch   72–75
  Fibers   94–97
  High Pass   58–59
  neutral   6
  Plastic Wrap   127
  Poster Edges   131
  Smart   60–62, 99
  Surface Blur   99
fine art   103–104
flat color layer, adding shading to   133
Foreground color   49–50
Foreground/Background Jitter setting   107
Freaky Details technique   98–99
full-spectrum image, for blend mode
  comparison   28–29

G

Gaussian blur
  adding to noise layer   91
  adding to SO   86–87
  gentle rain technique and   95, 97
  for graphic illustrations   82–83
  increasing edge contrast   45
  to lighten eyes   39
  in line sketches   72–73
  for portrait tone   68–69
  for retro outlines   129
  soft-glow effect with   78–79
gentle rain techniques   94–97
geometric patterns, Hard Mix mode for   166
Georgenes, Chris   117
Gilbert, Kat   103
gloss, in illustrations   127
glow effect, custom   88–89
glowing dust effect   119–121
Gradient brush setting   178
Gradient Editor, zone control and   56–57

Gradient tool
    checkerboard patterns with 128
    crosshatch textures with 130
    removing vignettes and 49–50
    retro outlines with 129
    set to Difference mode 115
    squares pattern with 131
graphic illustrations 82–83
gray day recovery 46–48
gray layer
    adding noise to 91
    in depth maps 113–114
    Dodge and Burn and 40
    in gentle rain technique 94–97
    Hue/Saturation adjustment with 70
gray value, in Multiply mode 139
grayscale versions, of blend mode outputs 19
Grid Luminosity blend mode, for 3D images 104

H

halftone noise effect 91–93
halo effects, of High Pass filter 59
hand tinting 71
Hard Light blend mode
    for 3D images 104
    adding color/texture with 67
    features/functions of 162
    for illustrated gloss 127
    Overlay mode comparison 160
    in sharpening images 58
Hard Mix blend mode 21
    creating vignettes and 54–55
    features/functions of 166
    increasing contrast with 90
    noise technique 91–93
    soft-glow effect with 84–85
Healing brush setting 178
Heaps, Mark 43
High Pass layer
    opacity and 14
    sharpening images 45, 58–59

highlights
    Hard Light mode for 162
    translucency in 161
History Brush setting 178
Hollywood, Calvin 99
Hue blend mode
    for 3D images 104
    Black & White adjustment layer and 71
    features/functions of 172
Hue Jitter setting, for custom brushes 107
Hue/Saturation adjustment
    for checkerboard patterns 128
    enhancing images with 44
    with gray layer 70
    increasing edge contrast 45
    for portrait tone 68–69
    for soft-glow effect 78–79
    zone control with gradients and 56
Hue/Saturation dialog box 30

I

illustrations
    applying textures to 116–118
    classic shading in 124–126
    color highlights for 108–111
    gloss in 127
    Soft Light mode for 133
Image noise. *See* noise
Inner Glow effect, in Layer Style dialog
    box 24–25
inverted blends
    black in 169
    brightness in 162, 175
    complementary colors with 164
    with Lighten mode 155
    muted 174
    reducing saturation for 160
Inverted self-blend 15
inverting colors 141
inverting duplicate image, in line sketches
    74–75

K

Kloskowski, Matt   37
Kost, Julieanne   65

L

LaMontagne, Patrick   133
layer blending
    Brush tool and   20–22
    tools for   22–24
layer groups, blend modes assigned to   98–99,
    176
Layer Style dialog box
    Blend If section in   23–24
    style selections in   24–25
layer(s)
    adjusting   16
    comparing/aligning   167
    styles, blend modes and   14
Layers panel, Pass Through mode in   18–19
lens flair effect, custom   88–89
Lighten blend mode
    for crosshatch textures   130
    features/functions of   155
lightening eyes   39
Lighter Color blend mode   159
line sketches   72–75
Linear Burn blend mode
    for 3D images   104
    features/functions of   152
    for graphic illustrations   82–83
    in line sketches   72–73
Linear Dodge blend mode
    features/functions of   158
    in line sketches   74–75
    Outer Glow set to   119–121
    in underexposure recovery   46
Linear Light blend mode
    features/functions of   164
    for random textures   122–123

Linear Light layer
    for 3D images   104
    changing opacity on   14
Lock Transparency, Behind/Clear modes
    and   177
luminance, with Linear Dodge mode   158
Luminosity blend mode
    for 3D images   104
    adjusting with gradients   56–57
    applied to Curves adjustment   15, 63
    Color mode comparison   174, 175
    enhancing images with   43–44
    features/functions of   175
    for soft-glow effect   84–85

M

Marquee tool, for illustrations   124–126
mask, applied to Normal mode   146
material, in 3D modeling   113
mathematics of blend modes   139
Merged setting, in Layer pop-up   51–53
microscopy, Divide mode for   170
monochrome images, Color mode for   70, 174
Move tool
    adding second image   76–77
    scrolling through modes   67
Multiply blend mode
    as default mode   24
    features/functions of   37, 150
    gentle rain technique with   97
    graphic illustrations with   82–83
    to lighten eyes   39
    mathematics of   139
    overlapping strokes and   21
    soft-glow effect and   78–79

N

nested groups, Pass Through mode for   176
neutral color, labeling of   138
neutral filters   6

Nik Silver Efex Pro 2   61–62
noise
    adjustment layer   81
    Dissolve mode and   147
    with Hard Mix   91–93
noise gradients, for crosshatch textures   130
Non-commutative label, blend mode   138
nondestructive layer-based tools   14
Normal blend mode
    for 3D images   104
    adding color/texture with   67
    Brush tool and   21
    features/functions of   146
    for soft-glow effect   84–85
Normal layer, Orton effect and   16–17

O

opacity
    blend mode sensitivity to   14
    Linear Burn mode and   152
    Orton effect and   16–17
    SO adjustment of   26–27
Opacity setting
    balancing contrast with   90
    blending layers with   22
    Brush tool   19–21
    in gentle rain technique   97
    glowing dust effect with   119–121
    illustrated textures with   116–118
    in Normal mode   146
    reducing blending with   16
    removing color cast   38
    soft-glow effect with   78–79
Orton effect
    combining blends for   16–18
    stacking transparencies for   79
Outer Glow effect
    for glowing lines/dust   119–121
    in Layer Style dialog box   24–25
outputs, blend mode   19

overlapping strokes   20–22
Overlay blend mode
    adding color/texture with   67
    color illustrations with   109
    creating vignettes   54–55
    Dodge and Burn and   40
    features/functions of   37, 160
    glowing dust effect with   119–121
    illustrated textures with   116–118
    to lighten eyes   39
    for portrait tone   68–69
    for sharp details   98–99
Overlay layer, in Orton effect   16–17

P

Paint Bucket brush setting   178
paint strokes
    blend modes with   20–22
    creating custom brushes for   105–107
    in dodge and burn   40–41
    effects created with   16
Painting blend   15
Pass Through blend mode
    combining blends with   18–19
    features/functions of   176
Pattern Stamp brush setting   178
patterns
    checkerboard   128
    Hard Mix mode for   166
    random   122–123
    retro outlines   129
    squares   131
Pen tool, for illustration shading   124–126
percentages, color inversion and   141
permanency, of overlapping strokes   20
photo restoration, Color mode for   174
Photoshop filters   6
Pin Light blend mode   165
pixelated edges   86–87
Plastic Wrap filter   127

portrait tone/contrast   68–69
Poster Edges filter, for squares pattern   131
Posterize adjustment layer   131
pseudo-halftone noise effect   91–93
Purity setting, for custom brushes   107

R

Radial Gradient tool
   removing vignettes   49–50
   set to Difference mode   115
   for squares pattern   131
Radius slider, sharpening images and   58
rain techniques   94–97
random noise pattern   147
random patterns/textures   122–123
reference images
   building   27–30
   understanding   139–142
removing color cast   38
removing vignettes   49–50
retouching techniques
   Calculations tool for   51–53
   Curves adjustments for   63
   Dodge and Burn   40–42
   edge contrast   45
   gray day recovery   46–48
   lightening eyes   39
   Luminosity for   43–44
   removing color cast   38
   removing vignettes   49–50
   restoring/creating vignettes   54–55
   sharpening images   58–59
   Smart Filters for   60–62
   zone control with gradients   56–57
retro outlines   129
RGB color model
   bit depth and   139
   in reference images   27–30

S

saturation
   of base color   172
   of blend color   173, 174
   in Color Dodge mode   157
   in Overlay mode   160
Saturation blend mode
   applied to Curves adjustment   63
   features/functions of   173
scatter brush, for glowing dust effect   119–121
Screen blend mode
   features/functions of   37, 156
   to lighten eyes   39
   sharpening images and   59
   soft-glow effect with   78–79
Screen layer, in Orton effect   16–17
Selection blend   15
self-blend overlay, for portraits   68–69
self-blends
   black in   167, 169
   full saturation in   163
   increasing contrast for   162, 164
   increasing saturation for   160
   Linear Burn mode and   152
   white in   170
sepia tone
   Color blend mode for   70
   hand-tinted   71
shading techniques
   with Dodge and Burn   127
   for illustrations   124–126
   translucency in   161
shadows   161, 162
Shannon, John   109
Shape Dynamics option, for custom
      brushes   107
Shape tool   179
Sharpen brush setting   178
Sharpen layer, Hard Light mode and   58

sharpening images
  High Pass filter for   58–59
  Smart Filters' blend modes for   60–62
sketch techniques   72–75
Smart Filters, blend mode controls of   60–62
Smart Objects (SOs)
  advantages of   26–27
  converting duplicate images to   69, 74–75
  Dissolve blend mode for   86–87
  Freaky Details technique and   99
  sharpening images and   58–59
Smudge Stick filter, for illustrated
    textures   116–118
Smudge tool
  blend modes with   178
  for color illustrations   109
  for custom lens flair effect   88–89
Snapping, in View menu   115
soft colors, with Lighten mode   155
Soft Light blend mode
  3D images and   104
  adding color/texture with   67
  color illustrations with   108–111
  features/functions of   37, 161
  in gentle rain technique   95
  light/shadow with   133
  to lighten eyes   39
soft-glow effect
  combining blends for   16–18
  Soft Glow 1 technique   78–79
  Soft Glow 2 technique   84–85
SOs. See Smart Objects (SOs)
special effects, with Pin Light mode   165
Spectrum gradient, for retro outlines   129
Sponge tool
  blend modes with   179
  destructive blending in   14
Spot Healing brush setting   178
Spread setting, for glowing dust effect
  119–121

squares pattern technique   131
Strength levels, in gentle rain technique   95
Subtract blend mode   169
Surface Blur filter, for sharp details   99

T

Tarantino, Chris   51
Texture brush setting   178
texture(s)
  in 3D modeling   113
  blend modes adding   66–67
  creating random   122–123
  crosshatch   130
  Darken mode for   148
  Divide mode for   76–77
  Hard Light mode for   127
  Hard Mix mode for   166
  in illustrations   116–118
This Layer option
  in Blend If section   23–24, 95
  trapping transparency   80
Threshold blend mode   146. See also Normal
  blend mode
Tierney, Jim   122
tinted color images, Color mode for   174
tone
  Color/Hue blend modes for   70
  for portraits   69
tool blend modes   177
translucency, with Soft Light mode   161
transparency
  Behind/Clear modes and   177
  Blend If sliders adjusting   16
  in Normal mode   146
  trapping   80
Transparent Stripes gradient, for squares
    pattern   131
Transparent Stripes preset, for checkerboard
    patterns   128

U

underexposure, recovery from 46–48
Underlying Layer option
  in Blend If section 23–24
  for soft-glow effect 78–79

V

Variance levels, in gentle rain technique 95
vector-based backgrounds 116–118
Vibrance adjustment, for enhancing
    images 44
vignettes
  removing 49–50
  restoring/creating 54–55
virtual output, of blend modes 5–7

Vivid Light blend mode
  color illustrations with 108–111
  features/functions of 163
  Freaky Details and 99
  retro outlines with 129

W

white color
  creating vignettes 54–55
  custom lens flair effect with 88–89
  glowing lines/dust with 119–121
  to lighten images 40
  in low-contrast images 90

Z

zone control with gradients 56–57

WHERE IDEAS
TAKE FLIGHT.

iStock has the perfect
photo, illustration, video
or music file for any idea.
So go ahead, aim high.

www.iStockphoto.com